must-see
IRELAND

D1809896

CONTENTS

Published by Thomas Cook Publishing
The Thomas Cook Group Ltd
PO Box 227, Thorpe Wood
Peterborough PE3 6PU
United Kingdom

Telephone: 01733 503571
E-mail: books@thomascook.com

ISBN 1 841570 70 2

Distributed in the United States of America by the Globe Pequot Press,
PO Box 480, Guilford, Connecticut 06437, USA.

Distributed in Canada by Whitecap Books, 351 Lynn Avenue,
North Vancouver, British Columbia, Canada V7J 2C4.

Distributed in Australia and New Zealand by Peribo Pty Limited,
58 Beaumont Road, Mt Kuring-Gai, NSW, 2080, Australia.

Publisher: Stephen York
Commissioning Editor: Deborah Parker
Map Editor: Bernard Horton

Series Editor: Christopher Catling

Written and researched by: Eric Bailey, Ruth Bailey and Donna Dailey

Cover photograph: Christopher Hill Photographic

must-see

IRELAND

**ERIC BAILEY,
RUTH BAILEY
and DONNA DAILEY**

Getting to know Ireland

Discovering Ireland

Few people arrive in Ireland without some ready-made notions, for the reputation of this small island nation in the North Atlantic is surprisingly strong around the world. Some visitors come on retreat, seeking relaxation in the quiet country lanes and timeless seaside villages, others on a trendy weekend break in the booming capital. Some come on pilgrimage to the ancient holy places of Christian saints, still others on a quest for the homeland of their ancestors. Whatever the image, it is certainly not detached, for Ireland is an emotive place with as many facets of culture and history as the forty shades of green in its landscape.

The land

This island, which is 303 miles (488km) long and 189 miles (304km) at its widest point, has an amazing diversity of terrain. Geographically, it is somewhat like a basin, with mountains rising up around the rim and a limestone plain in the centre which is alternately flat and rolling, broken by low hills, called drumlins, and numerous lakes. Much of the land is agricultural, fed by meandering rivers and divided by thick hedgerows or drystone walls. The most unique feature of Ireland's landscape is the vast stretches of blanket bog that cover much of the central and northwestern counties, a sight all the more startling when you learn that this country was once covered in thick oak forests. Ireland has the longest river, the Shannon, and the largest lake, Lough Neagh, in the British Isles, as well as the highest sea cliffs in Europe.

Emerald Isle

It's not, however, the turquoise blue of the lakes, the purple grey of the mountains or the tawny gold pelt of the boglands at sunset that is most frequently used to describe Ireland. This is, after all, the Emerald Isle, and it is the spectrum of greens you most remember, from dark and lush to shimmering with an almost electric brightness. The price to be paid for all this green is rain, and you should be prepared for sudden changes in the weather. However, the climate is moderated by the Gulf Stream, allowing fuchsias and even palms to flourish in sheltered spots.

Hospitality

Irish humour and wit are legendary, and ordinary people express themselves with great imagination and insight. No place in Ireland is without a story, and a lyrical one at that. People know and respect their history, for the sense of place and belonging to the land is inherent in the Irish character, a fact that makes the tragedies of the past all the more poignant. 'You are very welcome' is the greeting you'll receive in an Irish home, for their hospitality is second to none, a custom that dates back to Celtic times when such behaviour to travellers was a matter of honour.

Life in Ireland

There have been problems in the past – bitter strife, violence, economic depression – but Ireland today is a cheerful, buoyant place. Dublin, the capital of the Republic, is a boom town full of Irish rovers, many of whom have returned home to enjoy the good life they once sought abroad. Belfast, enjoying the fruits of peace after decades of 'The Troubles', is full of youthful optimism.

Home again

Ireland has seen its population growing again after decades of decline. Before the Great Famine of the 1840s the country's population was more than 6.5 million, but deaths from starvation and successive waves of emigration took such a toll that by 1961 there were only 2.8 million people in Ireland. Only a few years ago, Irish unemployment was among the highest in Europe. Today, spurred on by investment from the European Union, which Ireland joined in 1992, and foreign multinationals that have created new jobs, Ireland can boast the fastest growing economy in the industrialised world. It has been christened the 'Celtic Tiger', and its roar has reversed the tide of economic emigration for the first time in decades – Irish men and women are now returning home, or not even leaving in the first place, as they used to do.

The buzz

Today, Ireland is home to about 5 million happy-go-lucky souls (3.5 million in the Republic and 1.5 million in Northern Ireland) who are clearly enjoying every moment of their country's success. They're a comparatively young lot: 44 per cent of Ireland's population is under the age of 25. Dublin and Belfast, with their universities and thriving high-tech industries, have an even higher proportion of young people.

It certainly shows. Dublin's Grafton Street buzzes with the excitement of people eager to spend. Temple Bar, with its funky murals and Left Bank ambience, is electric from the determination of people to have fun. And in a typically Irish way, young Dubliners manage to be both dynamic and laid-back at the same time.

Music and song

They're a laconic bunch – dismissive of pomposity and pretentiousness – but they show the honest enjoyment of a child in their appreciation of the city's buskers, clowns and pavement artists. They work hard at their city jobs, but lunchtime is sacrosanct and the pubs become noisily filled. The conversations, refreshingly, are about the gigs they attended last weekend, what they'll be doing tonight and the party they'll be going to on Saturday, rather than company closures and redundancy pay-offs.

The 'craic'

The pubs fill up again in the evening, the best time to see the Irish at play. This is when they get together to enjoy 'the craic', that indefinable Irish phenomenon that means rather more than simply having a good time. Completely

uninhibited, they'll join in a song – or get up and sing one themselves – at the drop of a hat, and they're always ready for a good-natured discussion on any subject you care to raise. Well, almost any …

Yesterday and tomorrow

A branch of the Celts called the Gaels arrived in Ireland in the 6th century BC. Intermixing with the native Irish, they established cultural and legal systems that became the basis for Irish society and lasted into the 17th century. With the coming of St Patrick in AD 432, Christianity soon became the dominant faith of the land. While the rest of Christian Europe floundered during the Dark Ages, Ireland's monasteries blossomed as centres of art and learning. But God could not deliver Ireland from the Vikings, who landed in 795. The Norsemen established the country's first large towns, Dublin, Limerick, Wexford and Cork among them. In 1014, they were finally defeated by Ireland's first high king, Brian Ború.

Ireland's greatest conqueror did not invade but was invited in. In 1169 the king of Leinster, Dermot MacMurrough, sought help from Anglo-Norman mercenaries in regaining his lands. Their leader was the Earl of Pembroke, known as Strongbow, who, following his success in battle, went on to gain control of three-quarters of Ireland.

Rebellion and famine

English rule was to develop in ways that were antagonistic to the Catholic population. Discrimination fuelled the demand for Irish independence, which rose to a head in the late 17th century. It was hoped that the joining of Ireland and England as a United Kingdom, on 1 January 1801, would bring stability, but calls for Irish sovereignty were as strong as ever. A new leader arose in Catholic lawyer Daniel O'Connell, 'the Liberator', who swept to victory in the elections of 1828. Within a few years, however, thoughts of independence were put aside as Ireland suffered at the hands of the 1845 potato blight, which wiped out the crop that was the staple diet for the

majority of Irish peasants. It struck again the following year, and in 1848 and 1849. More than a million people starved or died of disease, and nearly twice their number were forced to emigrate.

Civil war and independence

A limited Home Rule bill was finally passed in 1914, but the Orange Order, a militant Protestant group, pushed through an amendment that gave the six counties of Ulster the option to remain part of Great Britain. World War I further delayed implementation of the bill.

The resurrected Irish Republican Brotherhood and the Irish Volunteers planned a nation-wide uprising for Easter Monday, 24 April 1916. The rebels in Dublin held out for five days before surrendering. The 14 who had signed the independence proclamation were executed. Public opinion, which had been against the uprising, swung fervently in favour of these new martyrs.

Peace at last?

After years of bitter fighting, Britain proposed the creation of the Irish Free State in the south. On 18 April 1949 the Republic of Ireland, or Eire, at last broke free as an independent nation. The division of Ireland continues to plague Irish politics, however. In the 1970s, a revived IRA, bent on achieving a united Ireland, launched a campaign of bombings and shootings that spread to England. More than 20 000 people have been injured or killed in 'The Troubles', with atrocities committed on both sides. Yet the desire for peace among the majority of Irish people, North and South, is slowly winning out. In 1998, representatives of all the major parties hammered out a framework for a peace agreement, which was signed on Good Friday, a fitting day of accord for nearly a century of division.

People and places

The Irish are proud that with a population of little more than 5 million their country has had a tremendous influence on world literature, drama and popular music.

The writers

Generally regarded as the father of modern Irish literature, **Jonathan Swift** was born in Dublin in 1667. His birthplace in Hoey's Court, near Dublin Castle, no longer exists, but his bust can be found in St Patrick's Cathedral, Dublin, where he served as Dean from 1713 until his death in 1745. Swift's wittily savage pen set the pace for modern satire.

Master of the macabre, **Bram Stoker** (1847–1912), creator of Count Dracula, was born at Clontarf, a northeast suburb. He worked in Dublin Castle as a civil servant before turning to writing.

Although he spent much of his later years in London – to say nothing of Reading Gaol – **Oscar Wilde** (1854–1900) was born at 21 Westland Row and educated at Trinity College before gaining a scholarship to Magdalen College, Oxford. The playwright **George Bernard Shaw** (1856–1950) was born at 33 Synge Street, now restored as a typical Victorian middle-class home and opened as the Shaw Birthplace Museum.

That colossus of Irish poetry, **William Butler Yeats**, was born in 1865 at 5 Sandymount Avenue, in the southeastern suburbs. He and Lady Gregory founded the Irish Literary Theatre at the old Abbey Theatre in 1904. One of their associates in the project was another Dubliner, the playwright **J M Synge** (1871–1909), author of *The Playboy of the Western World*. Yet another playwright associated with the Abbey was **Sean O'Casey**, author of *Juno and the Paycock*, who died in England in 1964. He was born at 85 Upper Dorset Street in 1880.

James Joyce, born at 41 Brighton Square, Rathgar, in 1882, was educated at University College, Dublin. He never set foot in Ireland after 1912. His first book of prose, *Dubliners*, was published in 1914 – but they say his masterpiece, *Ulysses* (1922), set on 16 June 1904, presents such a precise picture of Dublin that if the city were flattened it could be rebuilt brick by brick from his descriptions.

Other Dubliners who have made their mark on the 20th-century literary scene include Elizabeth Bowen, Samuel Beckett, Patrick Kavanagh, Brian O'Nolan (aka Flann O'Brien) and, of course, Brendan Behan, the roarin' writer who took up James Mangan's challenges of drink and ink. Among those still bearing the literary torch are Roddy Doyle, John Banville, Derek Mahon, Eavan Boland and Seamus Heaney. Like Heaney, not all its writers have been native Dubliners, but they have embraced the city as warmly as it has embraced their success.

The musicians

It began in the 1960s with The Chieftains and The Dubliners, and their folk-music challenge was picked up and carried along a rocking, rolling Celtic road by Phil Lynott and Thin Lizzy. Others soon followed the trail, then set off on their own at a cracking pace: Bob Geldof and the Boomtown Rats, U2, Moving Hearts and The Pogues. In 1982 Clannad scored a hit with their *Theme from Harry's Game*, a strange, mystical lament with Gaelic lyrics. Milestones along the way include Sinéad O'Connor, Chris de Burgh, Enya, Hothouse Flowers, Something Happens!, The Cranberries, and – of course – current Celtic hits Riverdance and The Corrs.

Getting around

By air

There are good internal flight connections from Dublin to other regions. For flights to Cork, Kerry, Shannon, Galway and Sligo, contact **Aer Lingus**, *tel: 01 705 3333* in Ireland, *020 8899 4747* in London. For flights to Donegal and the Aran Islands, contact **Aer Arann**, *tel: 01 814 5240*.

Public transport

CIE is Ireland's national transportation company. It has an information desk at Dublin Airport. Its three subsidiaries provide bus and train services throughout the country.

Irish Rail (Iarnród Éireann), *tel: 01 836 6222*, operates trains to most cities and major towns. **Dublin Bus** (Bus Átha Cliath), *tel: 01 873 4222*, operates in the greater Dublin area, including parts of adjoining counties. There is a range of discount tickets available from the head office at 59 Upper O'Connell Street and at numerous bus ticket agencies.

Irish Bus (Bus Éireann), *tel: 01 836 6111*, has a nation-wide network of buses serving all cities and most towns and villages outside the Dublin area.

In **Northern Ireland** there are four main rail routes from Belfast Central Station, *tel: 028 9089 9411*. The region is also well served by a good bus network. For information on services outside Belfast, contact **Ulsterbus**, *tel: 028 9033 3000*. Note that Belfast has two main bus stations. For city services within the Belfast area, contact **Citybus**, *tel: 028 9024 6485*.

Train and bus information in the UK

To obtain train and bus information in the UK, contact **CIE**, *Vistec House, 185 London Road, Croydon, Surrey CR0 2RJ; tel: 020 8686 0994*.

AA Republic of Ireland:
tel: 0800 667788.
AA Northern Ireland:
tel: 0800 420420.
RAC Northern Ireland:
tel: 0800 828282.

Documents

All drivers will need a full driving licence or international driving permit. A provisional licence is not accepted. If you are bringing your own car, motorcycle or caravan to Ireland, you will need the motor registration book and a letter of authority if the registration is not in your name. You will also need a green card or insurance certificate that is valid for the Republic of Ireland.

Driving

Car hire

To hire a car, you must show a full, valid driving licence from your country of residence, which you must have held for at least two years without endorsement. Because of insurance restrictions, you must be over 23 and under 70. The minimum hiring age varies between companies, so always check in advance.

Most major companies allow you to take the car between the Republic and Northern Ireland, but always make sure so that you don't invalidate your insurance.

Automobile clubs

It is a good idea to join an automobile association before your trip to Ireland, as it can provide useful information and documents and may have reciprocal agreements with local clubs in the event of a breakdown. Contact: UK: Automobile Association (AA), *tel: 0990 500600* ; Royal Automobile Club (RAC), *tel: 0990 722722.*

Drivers with disabilities

The orange badge issued to drivers with disabilities in the United Kingdom is also recognised in Ireland, and should be displayed prominently when in use. For more information, contact the **Disabled Drivers' Association**, *Carmichael House, North Brunswick Street, Dublin 7; tel: 01 946 4266.*

Grazing the long acre

Sheep, cows and other livestock practise this time-honoured tradition throughout rural Ireland, so be prepared for them to wander on to the road. Be especially careful on twisting roads with blind curves.

Parking

Many towns operate a disc-parking scheme: these are scratch cards that you buy from nearby shops and newsagents for the designated time you intend to park.

15

Safe parking

The police have published A Short Guide to Tourist Security, *available free at major tourist offices. It shows the locations of car parks in Dublin, Cork, Limerick and other cities.*

Police

To contact the police (*garda*) in an emergency, dial 999. Local police numbers can be found in the telephone directory.

Road signs

Ireland's small country roads are scenic, but they can also be frustrating to navigate. Road signs are notoriously poor or misleading in rural areas, if they exist at all (many end up in the pubs). Others may be broken off or purposely twisted in the wrong direction. A detailed map is essential.

In most parts of the country, place-names are written in both English and Irish (Dublin, for example, is 'Baile Atha Cliath'), but in the Gaeltacht areas such as Connemara and Donegal, signs are only in Irish. A map that gives both names is useful. Don't be afraid to ask a local for directions if you get lost.

In the Republic of Ireland, the old 'T' (Trunk) and 'L' (Link) routes have been renumbered as 'N' (National) and 'R' (Regional) routes. You will see both old and new signs and map designations. However, the road number is often not given at all, and local people rarely refer to roads by a number; rather, it's 'the Cork road' or whatever. It is more useful to know the name of the next town you're heading for. At unmarked intersections, a general rule is to carry on straight-ahead unless a sign directs you otherwise.

Speed limits are given in miles. The old black-on-white fingerpost road signs give distances between towns in miles, but as Ireland has gradually converted to metric, the new white signs and all of the green signs give the distances in kilometres, with 'km' after the number.

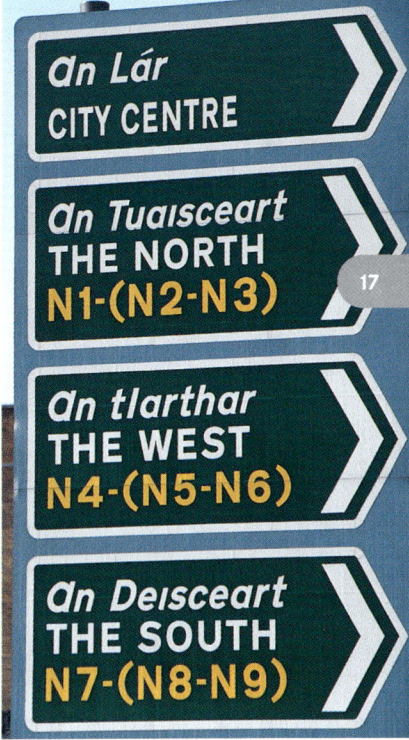

In Northern Ireland all distances are given in miles. Here, major roads have 'A' and minor roads 'B' designations, with 'M' for motorways.

Speed limits

Speed limits are 30mph (45kph) in towns unless signs indicate otherwise. The general speed limit on most roads is 60mph (95kph) unless otherwise posted. The motorway speed limit is 70mph (110kph).

Irish miles

You may notice the old granite milestones along road verges, especially in County Down, which are marked in Irish miles. An Irish mile measures 2 240 yards, which is 480 yards longer than an English mile. All modern road signs, however, give distances in standard English miles.

Don't miss

1 Dublin's Trinity College and the Book of Kells

Ireland's most famous medieval book, the richly decorated Book of Kells, dating from the 9th century, is the highlight of a visit to the treasure-packed Old Library in Ireland's foremost university. **Pages 50-1**

2 Bru na Boinne (Newgrange)

One of Europe's most important Neolithic (New Stone Age) sites, the Newgrange passage grave is 4 000 years old – more ancient, and every bit as impressive, as the pyramids of Egypt. **Pages 64-5**

3 Powerscourt House and Gardens

Explore 45 acres (18 hectares) of glorious formal and walled gardens nestling in the gentle Irish countryside. Walk the terraces, admire the statues and visit the 300ft (100m) waterfall on the River Dargle. **Page 75**

4 Cashel

From 5th-century seat of the Irish kings of Munster to flourishing medieval abbey, the rocky stronghold at Cashel is redolent of every phase of Ireland's long history. **Pages 92-3**

5 Waterford

Founded by Viking settlers in 853, Waterford is a characterful town, famous for its cut glass, and a great base for exploring the fishing villages and monastic sites of the south coast. **Pages 104-5**

6 Blarney Castle

Who has not heard of Blarney Castle's legendary stone, guaranteed to loosen the tongue and confer persuasive eloquence on anyone who kisses its damp surface?
Pages 118–19

19

7 Cork

Ireland's Bohemian second city, a place of merchants' warehouses and artists' studios, with an almost Dutch ambience. Pages 121–3

8 Dingle Peninsula

Escape the urban jungle to explore the fascinating remains of Irish religion, from pagan inscribed stones to the beehive-shaped huts of Christian monks and hermits. Pages 124–5

9 Bunratty Castle

You'll either love or hate the mock medieval banquets hosted by the adjacent folk park, but there's no denying the authenticity and power of Bunratty's formidable 15th-century castle.
Page 145

10 Giant's Causeway

Of Northern Ireland's numerous scenic coastal highlights, the Giant's Causeway wins the top prize for the sheer magic of its setting and the contrast between nature's wild confusion and the precise geometry of these honeycomb rocks.
Pages 212–13

Dublin

Dublin is one of the trendiest destinations in Europe. The Celtic Tiger has set the city roaring, generating new restaurants and a lively nightlife in such areas as Temple Bar.

the sea the sea crimson sometimes like fire

DUBLIN

BEST OF
Dublin

Getting there: **Dublin Airport** *(tel: 01 844 4900) is 6 miles (10km) north of the city centre. The Airlink Dublin bus service runs between the airport and the city centre, with stops at the central bus station (Busaras), Connolly Rail station and Heuston Rail station. Taxi fares are about £15. The ferry port for Dublin is at Dun Laoghaire (pronounced 'Dun-Leary'), 6 miles (10km) south of the city centre. It is accessible by bus or DART, and taxis also meet the ferries.*

North

to National Botanic Gardens

PHIBSBOROUGH

0 ··· 1/2 km
0 ··· 1/4 mile

Mater Misericordiae Hospital

North Circular Road

Berkeley Rd
Upper Dorset St

St Brendan's Hospital

North Circular Road

Phibsborough

Prussia St

Summerhill

Bus Station

Portland Row

Marmon St

Constitution Hill

Dublin Writers Museum

(4)

Parnell Sq East

James Joyce Centre

Connolly Station

St Laurence's Hospitals

North King St
North Bolton St
Capel Street

Parnell Street

O'Connell St

Cathedral

Bus Station

King Street

Blackhall Place

P.O.

Old Jameson Distillery

Mkt

General Post Office

Custom House

Custom House Quay

to Dublin Zoo

Collins Barracks

River Liffey

Parkgate Street

Wolfe Tone

Ellis Qy

Church Street

Arran Qy
Inns Qy
Ormond

Four Courts

Quay

Aston Qy

Pearse Street

North

Mount St Lower

Victoria Quay

Guinness Hop Store

Usher's Qy Merchant's Quay

Wood Qy

Wellington Qy

(3)

(8)

D'Olier St

(1)

Trinity College

National Library

(6)

Leinster House

James's Street

Thomas Street

West

High St

Christ Church Cath

Dame St

(2)

Dvblinia

(5)

Nassau St

Natural History Museum

(7)

St Patrick's Hospital

Iveagh Market

New St

St Patrick's St

St Patrick's Cathedral

Aungier St

Grafton St

Dawson St

Kildare St

St Stephen's Green

The Coombe

to Irish Museum of Modern Art and Kilmainham Gaol

Clanbrassil St Lwr

Camden St

Leeson St

National Concert Hall

Shaw's Birthplace

DOLPHIN

Charlemont St

Adelaide Road

DUBLIN

(1) Book of Kells

Ireland's most famous medieval book, the richly decorated illuminated manuscript from the 9th century, is housed inside Trinity's Old Library, with other priceless treasures from the past. **Page 51**

(2) *Dublin Castle*

Contrast the lavish State Apartments with the ruins of Dublin's original Viking fortress. **Pages 28–9**

(3) *Ha'penny Bridge*

Cross the River Liffey on Dublin's most enduring and endearing image, the elegantly bowed Wellington Bridge (to give it its official name when it opened in 1816), take in the views on either side and smile, as everyone does. **Page 34**

(4) *Hugh Lane Municipal Gallery of Modern Art*

Irish artists from Jack Yeats to Francis Bacon. **Page 35**

(5) Molly Malone

Pay your respects to the buxom fishmonger, *Molly Malone*, pushing her wheelbarrow on the corner of Grafton and Suffolk streets. **Page 33**

(6) *National Gallery*

Paintings and sculpture from every major European school. **Page 42**

(7) *National Museum*

Stunning Celtic artefacts and material from Ireland's prehistoric past as well as from more recent history. Continue your exploration of Ireland's past by visiting the 300-year-old Collins Barracks, the ideal new venue for thousands of exhibits which they couldn't fit into the city-centre museum. **Page 43**

(8) *Temple Bar*

Temple Bar might well have become a bus station; instead, it is Dublin's Left Bank, famous for *bijoux* restaurants and lively nightlife. **Page 49**

23

Tourist information

Dublin Tourist Information Office is housed in the deconsecrated St Andrew's Church on Suffolk Street, where you can book tickets, tours and hotels as well as pick up information. *Tel: 01 605 7787; e-mail: information@dublintourism.ie; reservations@dublintourism.ie; website: www.visit.ie/dublin*. There are additional tourist information offices at the Arrivals hall in Dublin Airport, the terminal building at Dun Laoghaire harbour and at Baggot Street Bridge, Dublin 2.

Chester Beatty Library and Gallery of Oriental Art

Bermingham Tower, Dublin Castle. Tel: 01 677 7129. Open: Mon–Fri 1000–1700, Sat–Sun and public holidays 1400–1700. ££.

Sir Alfred Chester Beatty died in 1968, bequeathing his magnificent collection of oriental furniture, decorated manuscripts, paintings and ceramics to the Irish nation. The priceless collection includes some of the earliest known biblical papyri as well as numerous early copies of the Koran. The collection is so large that curators estimate it will take 55 years to display everything in a rotating exhibition.

Christ Church Cathedral

Christchurch Place. Tel: 01 677 8099. Open: daily 1000–1730. £.

Dublin's first church was a simple wooden structure built on this site in 1038 by Sitric Silkenbeard, king of the Dublin Norsemen. The magnificent stone edifice that stands today is Dublin's oldest building, built from 1169 by Richard de Clare, Earl of Pembroke. The earl, who is buried here, was known as **Strongbow**, and he commanded the successful Anglo-Norman invasion of Ireland. Strongbow's wife's uncle, Archbishop Laurence O'Toole, played an important part in the design of the church and became Dublin's patron saint. His heart is preserved in a metal casket in St Laud's Chapel at the east end of the cathedral.

The first task was to dig out the huge **crypt**. Covering the entire area of the cathedral, the crypt survives as one of the largest in northern Europe and it houses many unusual relics, including a mummified cat and rat, found in an organ pipe during restoration.

> " *If a man is born in a stable, it doesn't mean he is a horse.* "
>
> **The Duke of Wellington, who was born in Dublin but who did not want to be considered Irish**

The **Great Nave**, 68ft (25m) high, was completed around 1220 and has some fine early Gothic arches. For centuries, the British establishment in Ireland used this as its principal place of worship. Richard II knighted four Irish kings here in 1395, and

Lambert Simnel (The Pretender) was crowned Edward VI of England in May 1487.

The cathedral went through a rough patch in 1562, when the roof collapsed, destroying the south arcade, most of the west front and Strongbow's tomb (later restored, using the effigy of a knight whose identity has long been forgotten). The **cloisters** became a market-place, and in the crypt 'tippling rooms' were established for drinking and smoking.

In 1821, Skinners' Row, later to be renamed Christchurch Place, was widened to show the cathedral to its best advantage. All it revealed, however, was that the building was on the verge of collapse. Henry Roe, a wealthy whiskey distiller, stepped in to underwrite the cost of reconstruction.

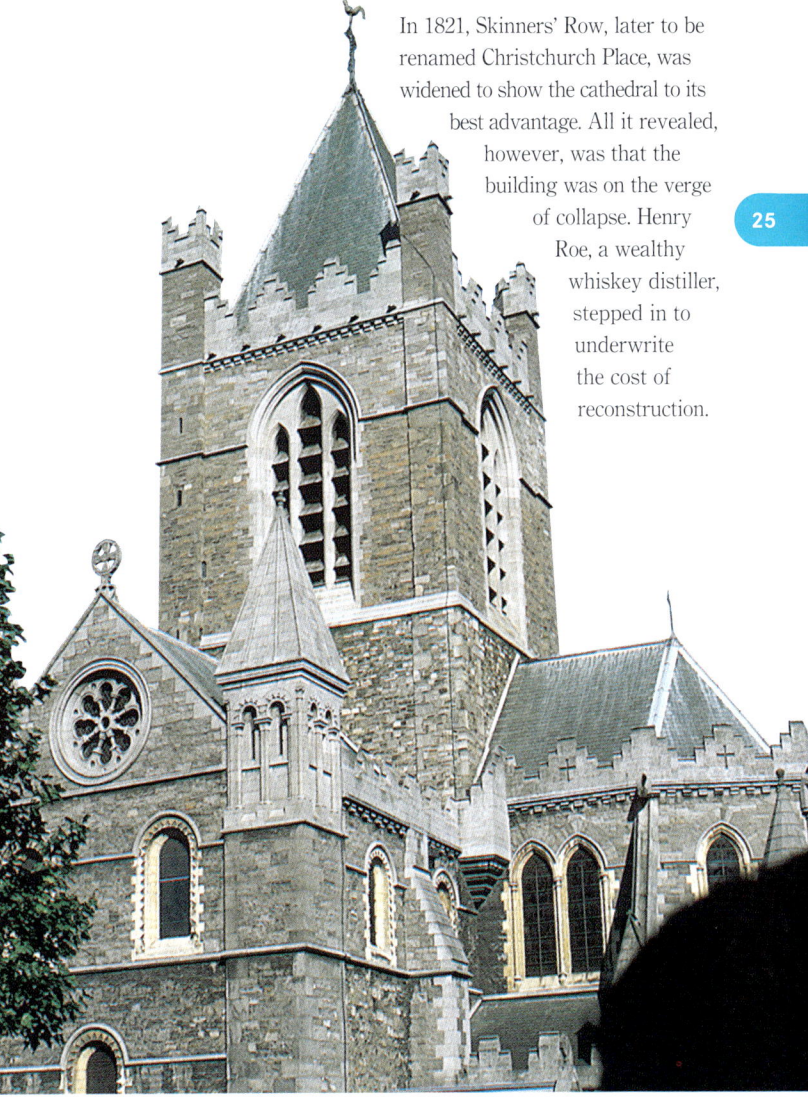

Collins Barracks

Benburb Street. Tel: 01 677 7444. Open: Tue–Sat 1000–1700, Sun 1400–1700. £.

Set on an 18-acre (7-hectare) site, Collins Barracks dates from 1701 and claims the distinction of being Europe's oldest military barracks and the world's oldest continuously occupied barracks – almost 300 years. In 1994 the property was acquired by the **National Museum of Ireland**. It now houses weaponry, decorative arts and countless other fine exhibits on two floors. Visitors can see a 2 000-year-old Japanese ceremonial bell, gauntlets worn by King William at the Battle of the Boyne (1690) and Wolfe Tone's pocket book, which he kept with him during his incarceration at the barracks in 1798 – the year of the Rebellion.

In 1985 a **monument** was erected at the barracks where men who were executed for their part in the Rebellion are buried. Formerly known as the Royal Barracks, the imposing building of Wicklow granite was renamed after Michael Collins, the revolutionary who was killed in the civil war in 1922.

Designs on Dublin

James Gandon, born in 1742, was a successful London architect in his thirties, poised to go to the Russian city of St Petersburg to work on a major project, when another invitation drew him to Dublin to build a new Custom House. He was to spend the rest of his days in Ireland, becoming the architect of some of the city's most prestigious buildings, including the Four Courts – Chancery, King's Bench, Exchequer and Common Pleas – at Inns Quay, and Parliament House on College Green (opposite the entrance to Trinity College), which has been used as the head office of the Bank of Ireland since 1808.

Custom House

Custom House Quay. Tel: 01 878 7660. Open: mid-Mar–Nov, Mon–Fri 1000–1700, Sat–Sun 1400–1700; Nov–mid-Mar, Wed–Fri 1000–1700, Sun 1400–1700. £.

Splendidly impressive, especially when seen reflected in the still waters of the River Liffey, the magnificent neo-classical Custom House is Dublin's finest Georgian public building. It was designed by the master architect **James Gandon** and completed in 1791, replacing a building at Wellington Quay and creating a place where cargoes could be loaded and unloaded close to the city's commercial centre. Many people involved in commerce opposed the new site nearer the mouth of the river and hired mobs to attack the builders.

Its gleaming façade of Portland stone stretches 374ft (114m) from end to end. A copper dome rises behind the central portico, crowned by a statue of Commerce. The interior was badly damaged when Republicans set fire to the building in 1921, and it only reopened after extensive restoration in time for the Custom House's bicentenary in 1991. It is now used for government offices, but there is a **visitor centre** in the dome and clock tower area that is open daily to the public. Here the building's history is outlined, and displays focus on Gandon and his life and work in Ireland. The best view of the building is from the south side of the Liffey, particularly when lit at night.

Dublin Castle

Dame Street. Tel: 01 677 7129. Open: Mon–Fri 1000–1700, Sat–Sun and Bank Holidays 1400–1700. ££.

Archaeologists have found evidence of a defensive rath or earthwork that existed on the site of Dublin Castle even before the Vikings arrived and built their fortress in 841. Both early fortifications were sited on a strategic ridge at the confluence of the River Liffey and its tributary, the Poddle. Here the two rivers formed a black pool, or *dubh linn* in Irish, which gave the city its name.

King John ordered a **new castle** to be built in 1204, and the first stage, consisting of a central circular keep and a curtain wall with massive towers, was completed around 1215. The keep survives as the **Record Tower**. Total reconstruction began after 1684 when fire destroyed the vice-regal quarters. The **Chapel Royal** was built between 1807 and 1814. From the mid-19th century the castle served as headquarters of the Dublin Metropolitan Police and housed the vice-regal offices and State apartments. It was handed over to the new Irish Government in 1922. The castle's **main gate**, at the top end of Cork Hill, off Dame Street, is surmounted by Van Nost's *Statue of Justice* which, Dubliners wryly observe, has its back turned on the city.

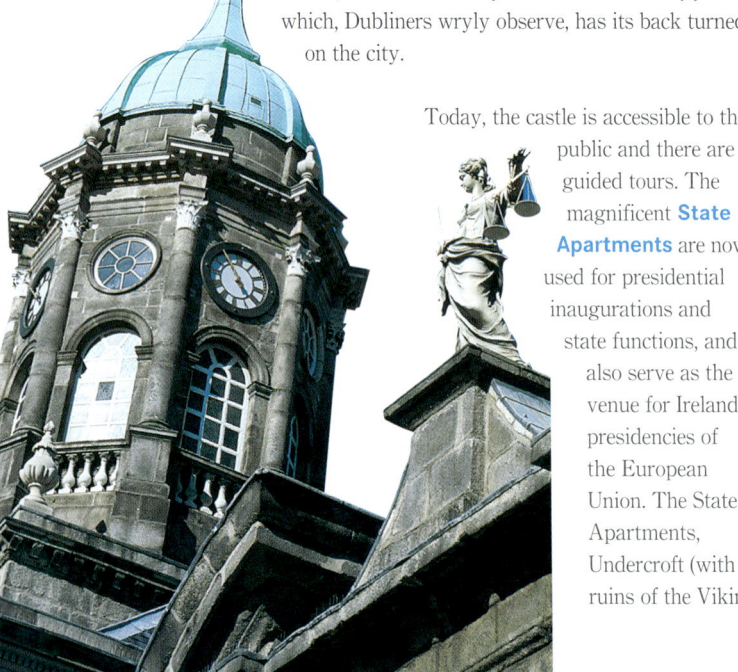

Today, the castle is accessible to the public and there are guided tours. The magnificent **State Apartments** are now used for presidential inaugurations and state functions, and also serve as the venue for Ireland's presidencies of the European Union. The State Apartments, Undercroft (with ruins of the Viking fortress) and the Gothic Revival Chapel Royal are normally open to visitors, but the State Apartments may be closed on occasions for State purposes.

Dublin Writers Museum

18 Parnell Square North. Tel: 01 872 2077. Open: Mon–Sat 1000–1700 (to 1800 weekdays Jun–Aug); Sun and public holidays 1100–1700. ££.

Housed in a splendid Georgian mansion on the north side of Parnell Square, this museum commemorates the lives and works of the *crème de la crème* of Dublin's literary world. You can peruse the letters, diaries, photographs and mementoes that inspired Swift, Wilde, Beckett, Joyce and Shaw, to name a few. The house, former home of John Jameson (the whiskey producer), is elegantly restored, particularly the **Gallery of Writers**, and features magnificent plasterwork and stained-glass windows. Readings are sometimes held here.

Dublin Zoo

Phoenix Park. Tel: 01 677 1425; fax: 01 677 1660. Open: Mon–Sat 0930–1800, Sun 1030–1800 (last admission 1700). £££.

Thirty acres (12 hectares) of Phoenix Park are home to animals from many parts of the world. Dublin Zoo, established around 1831, is thought to be the third oldest in the world. It is known for its rare and endangered animals and for its breeding programmes. One of its major successes is the breeding of lions in captivity, and the famous MGM lion was born in Dublin Zoo.

An educational discovery centre, a daily 'Meet the Keeper' opportunity, feeding programmes, a children's corner with pigs, sheep, goats and fluffy guinea pigs, train rides and a children's play area are popular features.

Gibbons, chimpanzees, orang-utans and spider monkeys cavort on Monkey Islands in the lakes. The World of Cats presents African and Asian species, and polar bears and other animals and birds in the Arctic section are a big draw.

Dvblinia

St Michael's Hill, Christ Church. Tel: 01 679 4611. Open: Apr–Sept, daily 1000–1700; Oct–Mar, Mon–Sat 1100–1600, Sun 1000–1630. ££.

Housed in the Synod Hall, which is linked to Christ Church Cathedral by a picturesque bridge, Dvblinia starts with a multimedia presentation tracing the development of the city from the arrival of the Anglo-Normans to Tudor times in the 16th century. Ten scenes from Dublin's medieval history are re-created in sets and tableaux. The museum area has artefacts recovered from the Wood Quay archaeological site, where the Norsemen founded their first settlement in 841. A panoramic view over Dublin can be had from atop St Michael's Tower.

Dublin's Viking Adventure

Essex Street West. Tel: 01 679 6040. Open: Tue–Sat 1000–1630. ££.

Dublin wasn't much more than a hamlet when the Vikings arrived in 841. The newcomers lost no time in building fortifications and a harbour, then set about pillaging other parts of Ireland, using their new colony as a base.

Compared with the Irish, who until now had been enjoying their 'golden age' of monasticism, the Norsemen were uncouth, uneducated brutes, but they were able to hold the native population down through lack of unified resistance. The Vikings were great traders, especially in slaves, and Dublin developed into a port and market-place.

The city savoured a brief spell without foreign rule when the Vikings, quarrelling among themselves, were driven out by a rare unity of Irish forces. By 917, however, they were back. This time, they concentrated on developing Dublin as a major fortified trading centre. They built Wood Quay on the south side of the Liffey and constructed permanent homes and other buildings in the surrounding area.

You can get an idea of what life was like in Viking Dublin at **Dublin's Viking Adventure**, a fanciful trip through time which re-creates the sights, sounds and even smells of old 'Dyflin', as the Vikings knew it. The final section of the trip features an important collection of artefacts discovered in excavations at nearby Wood Quay and other parts of Viking Dublin.

General Post Office

O'Connell Street. Tel: 01 705 7000. Open: Mon–Sat 0800–2000, Sun 1000–1830.

This striking public building, designed by the neo-classical architect Francis Johnston and built between 1814 and 1818, is famous in Irish history as the headquarters of the

Republican rebels during the **1916 Easter Rising**. From its steps, Patrick Pearse read out the Proclamation of the Republic of Ireland. Most of the original building was destroyed in the subsequent shelling, though the façade survived, and you can still see bullet holes in the portico columns. After restoration it reopened in 1929 and it remains the city's main post office today. Step inside for a look at the handsome interior.

The Easter Rising

The Irish Volunteer Force was set up in Dublin in 1913 to defend Ireland's claim to Home Rule. The vast majority of the Irish Volunteers, however (about 200 000), were persuaded to fight in the Great War (World War I) against the Germans. This left only about 10 000 to act as a national defence force. It was decided to organise a rising while Britain was busy fighting against Germany. The proclamation of a republic was read outside the GPO on Easter Monday, 1916.

Many O'Connell Street buildings were severely damaged in the fierce battle that followed. In less than a week, under heavy attack from British troops and with many civilian casualties, the rebels had to surrender. Fourteen of the leaders of the Rising were executed within three weeks of that Easter Monday bloodbath.

Grafton Street

Dublin throbs to the sound of music, and nowhere more so than in Grafton Street. A stroll along the thoroughfare, pedestrianised since 1988, is like a visit to a rock and folk festival, with solo performances by traditional and classical musicians thrown in for good measure.

> " *In Dublin, the definition of an introvert could be someone who has never busked on Grafton Street.* "
>
> **Dublin Tourism in *Rock 'n' Stroll*, a guide to the city's Music Trail.**

Music, music, music!

A coin tossed into a hat or fiddle case is all you're expected to pay for a gig by someone whose name may well be known world-wide the day after tomorrow. It's happened before – and more than once. Five of the 16 plaques along the Rock 'n' Stroll Trail honouring the city's musicians and singers are to be found on or very near Grafton Street. This is where ex-Trinity College student Chris de Burgh once wowed passers-by, as did the Hothouse Flowers, a group as Gaelic as Ireland itself. **Bewley's Café**, that hothouse of tea-table gossip, was an unlikely launch pad for the success of Bob Geldof and the Boomtown Rats. The café, as middle-class as a coffee morning, was a regular meeting place for the band, and it was here that its hit single *Rat Trap* was created.

The pubs

There's no shortage of watering holes along Grafton Street, and no fear of boredom as you swig a pint of the black stuff or sip a ball o' malt (glass of whiskey). Literary figures – fact, fictitious, famous, dead or aspiring – are a feature of almost every bar. **The Bailey**, 2 Duke Street, was frequented by James Joyce before he left Ireland's shores in 1912. **Davy Byrne's**, across the street at No 21, owes some of its fame to the fact that Leopold Bloom, hero of Joyce's *Ulysses*, dropped by for a snack on 16 June 1904 – now celebrated annually as Bloomsday. Nearby **McDaid's**, 3 Harry Street, is the quintessential Dublin pub, a fact which endeared it to its most famous client, the playwright and ex-Borstal boy Brendan Behan.

Shopping cornucopia

The conventional way to enter the Grafton Street area is to cross the Nassau Street/Suffolk Street intersection, passing a wink at **Molly Malone** as you go. An alternative route from the Dublin Tourism Centre on Suffolk Street, however, is to continue along St Andrew Street and into William Street South. The **Powerscourt Townhouse Centre** is best entered through the splendid façade of the mansion that once stood here. The Centre is Dublin's most up-market shopping mall, containing a cornucopia of shops and eating places. There are shops selling everything from hiking gear to babywear and musical instruments. Richard, 3rd Viscount Powerscourt, for whom the elegant mansion was completed in 1774, would probably not be dismayed by the quality of the jewellery, crafts and fashion available through the Centre's 80 shops.

At the opposite end of the scale, nearby **George's Arcade**, a covered market reaching across to South Great George's Street, presents everything from fruit and vegetables to second-hand clothing and books, collectables and antiques.

Guinness Brewery and Hop Store

St James Gate. Tel: 01 408 4800. Open: Apr–Sept, Mon–Sat 0930–1700, Sun 1030–1630; Oct–Mar, Mon–Sat 0930–1600, Sun 1200–1600. £££.

The home of the world's most famous stout is also Dublin's most popular tourist attraction, even though the brewery itself is closed to the public. It was established by Arthur Guinness in 1759 at James Gate, west of Christ Church Cathedral, and as the popularity of the dark brew spread round the world, operations expanded to cover some 60 acres (24 hectares). The **Guinness Hop Store**, set in a 19th-century building on Crane Street, contains the 'World of Guinness' Exhibition, an advertising gallery displaying the company's famous campaign posters and, of course, a re-created Victorian pub where you can sample a pint of Dublin's finest.

Ha'penny Bridge

Officially it's the Wellington Bridge, named after the Duke of Wellington who died in 1852, but everybody knows it as the Ha'penny Bridge, so called because in days gone by this was the toll charged for crossing it. A beautiful structure with elegant lamps, it is one of the earliest cast-iron bridges in Ireland and is the only footbridge spanning the River Liffey, crossing between Bachelors Row and Wellington Quay.

Hugh Lane Municipal Gallery of Modern Art

Parnell Square North. Tel: 01 874 1903. Open: Tue–Thur 0930–1800 ('til 2000 on Thur Apr–Aug), Fri–Sat 0930–1700, Sun 1100–1700. £.

The grand Georgian interior of Charlemont House forms the backdrop for the gallery's collection of 20th-century Irish art. The work of Roderic O'Conor, Jack B Yeats, Walter Osborne and John Lavery are displayed alongside contemporary artists such as Kathy Prendergast, Dorothy Cross and Willie Doherty. The international collection includes Impressionist works and those of late 20th-century artists. Some of the paintings are exchanged with others in London's National Gallery every few years. There is also a sculpture hall and stained-glass work by Harry Clarke and Evie Hone. The studio of Francis Bacon, the gallery's latest bequest, will open in 2001.

The museum is named after its benefactor, **Hugh Lane**, who decided to donate his collection of Impressionist works to Dublin Corporation in 1905, with the proviso that they should be exhibited in a suitable building. The Corporation dragged its heels in finding an appropriate place, so Sir Hugh, losing patience, thought he would let London's National Gallery have the gift instead. Later he had second thoughts and attempted to revert to his original plan. He added a codicil to his will to this effect, but before it was witnessed, Sir Hugh met an untimely death – he was a passenger on the *Lusitania* when it was torpedoed in World War I. It took lawyers half a century to sort out the legacy, though nobody was entirely happy with the outcome, which was that Dublin and London should take turns to show the Impressionist collection. Each city has it for a few years at a time.

Irish Museum of Modern Art

Military Road, Dublin 8. Tel: 01 612 9900. Open: Tue–Sat 1000–1730, Sun 1200–1730. £.

The former Royal Hospital Kilmainham is now home to a museum that presents an exciting range of contemporary Irish and international art. Drama and musical performances are also staged, and there are continuing community and educational programmes. The museum also has a coffee shop and bookshop.

The **Royal Hospital** opened in 1684 to accommodate 300 maimed and infirm soldiers. It was designed by the Irish Surveyor-General, Sir William Robinson, and was styled on *Les Invalides* in Paris, with a formal façade and an elegant courtyard. At first, people were so impressed by the building's beauty that it was suggested it should be used instead to house Trinity College, but it remained a hospital for almost 250 years. The building was restored by the Irish government in 1986 and needed only minimal alterations to accommodate the museum.

Iveagh Market

Northern end of Francis Street.

The Iveagh Market opened in 1907 and is housed in an intriguing Victorian building, with arches adorned by the carved heads of Moors and oriental traders. One carving, of a grinning and winking Occidental, is said to be that of Lord Iveagh himself, the man who established the market while he was head of the Guinness brewing family.

This part of Dublin, west of the two cathedrals and bounded by Francis Street and Thomas Street, forms a district known as **The Liberties**, a free-booting, devil-may-care area when it lay outside the old city walls – a tract of overcrowded, crime-ridden, festering slums by the end of the 18th century.

A parliamentary act of 1841 changed the city's administration and opened the door over the next 20 years for the abolition of the Liberties. Until recently, however, the change seemed to have been little more than a legality: the Liberties continued to be different and apart from the rest of Dublin, and to some extent they continue to be so to this day. Gentrification is encroaching on the narrow streets of small, red-brick houses, but there are still some parts where poverty is all too apparent.

It may be a development of the area's old insecurity, when second-hand goods and the pawnshops brought temporary relief, but whatever the reason, the Liberties is now noted for its antiques and craft items. **Francis Street** is the focal point for collectors and dealers. Here, you'll find shops selling old advertising boards and enamel signs, garden statuary, vintage fireplaces, pine furniture, lamps, medals and coins, and there are craftsmen to repair, clean or restore them.

James Joyce Centre

37

35 North Great George's Street. Tel: 01 878 8547. Open: Mon–Sat 0930–1700, Sun 1230–1700. ££.

Housed in a restored Georgian town house, the James Joyce Centre focuses on the life and works of one of Ireland's greatest authors. Along with the reference library and exhibition rooms, there are tours of the house, and museum staff lead walks through Joyce's old stomping grounds in this north section of the inner city. Joyce fans can also pick up the Ulysses Map of Dublin from the tourist information office, which points out related sights of interest.

Joyce believed that to write about a place you need to distance yourself from it – he lived most of his life abroad, yet always wrote about Dublin. *Ulysses*, his *magnum opus*, tells of a single Dublin day, as experienced by many local characters. The book was considered pornographic and remained on the banned list in Ireland until 1960.

DUBLIN

Kilmainham Gaol

Inchicore Road, Dublin 8. Tel: 01 453 5984. Open: Apr–Sept, daily 0930–1800 (last tour 1630); Oct–Mar, Mon–Fri 0930–1700 (last tour 1600), Sun 1000–1800 (last tour 1630). ££.

A grim island among quiet suburban streets, Kilmainham Gaol is a disquieting museum. It tells two stories: outlining penal reform towards the end of the 18th century and plotting the course of Ireland's struggle for independence from British rule.

When it opened in 1796 on a site disconcertingly known as Gallows Hill, Kilmainham Gaol was considered a **model prison**. Whether the prisoners would have agreed is a different matter: prison reformers at that time believed fresh air solved many problems, so the prisoners suffered from cold and damp as well as the psychological effects of almost solitary confinement. Soon, over-crowding became a burden, too.

After the 1798 Rebellion **political prisoners** joined the ordinary inmates, and in 1803, when Robert Emmet's

insurrection failed, some 200 rebels were jailed. Emmet himself was executed. The prison was enlarged, which merely provided the authorities with more room for the incarceration of independence activists. Many died at the hands of the public executioner; luckier ones were transported to Australia.

Famous prisoners

Perhaps the most shocking chapter in the gaol's history came in 1916 when 14 leaders of the Easter Rising (*see page 31*) were court-martialled and shot in the old stone-breakers' yard.

There were further shootings even after the inauguration of the Free State. In 1922, during the civil war, Republican opponents of the new government were executed as the 'martyrs' of 1916 had been.

The last political leader to be kept in the prison – indeed, he was the last prisoner of all – was **Eamon de Valera**, later to serve as Ireland's prime minister and president. Kilmainham closed with the release of de Valera on 16 July 1924. The old gaol was allowed to fall into decay, and by 1960 was a roofless ruin, when a group of veterans from the 1916 era decided it should be restored as a national monument. It took a force of volunteers more than 20 years to complete the restoration. Today, Kilmainham's cells are empty of prisoners, but full of poignancy.

Leinster House

Kildare Street. Not open to the public but can be viewed from the ornate entrance gates.

Leinster House was built in 1749 as a home for the Earl of Kildare, who later became Duke of Leinster. Today, this palatial house is home to the Dáil, the Irish Parliament. From the street, which is the closest most visitors can get without an invitation from a member of the Dáil, Leinster House looks more like an art gallery than the powerhouse of Irish politics – a symbolic notion, perhaps, since the Irish, more than anyone, have turned the hurly-burly of debate on any subject into an art form.

This is where the big issues of Irish life are mauled, if not settled, by 226 people. Politics in Ireland – whether national or international – can be entertaining, dramatic, historic, but never dull.

Irish democracy

The Republic of Ireland is governed as a parliamentary democracy with an upper and lower chamber – the Dáil (House of Representatives) and the Seanad (Senate). The President is head of state and the Taoiseach (Prime Minister) is head of the government.

Merrion Square

If a Roman Catholic archbishop had not changed his mind, the magnificent Georgian houses in Merrion Square would have been overshadowed by a cathedral instead of facing each other grandly across some 12 acres (5 hectares) of attractive parkland. Church authorities had held the land for many years, intending it as the site for a cathedral, but in 1974 Archbishop Ryan handed it back to the city.

The square was laid out in 1752 by John Ensor for the 2nd Viscount Fitzwilliam of Merrion, who wanted to lure Dublin's uppercrust families to the south side of the river. The original **houses** are still standing, and handsome they are, too, with their ornate front doors and fanlights, brass knockers and intricate wrought-iron balconies. Winding evergreen paths lead to a central **green** with lovely flower gardens featuring a number of **sculptures**. Among them is a bust of *Henry Grattan* by Peter Grant and the figure of *Èire* by Jerome Connor. *Tribute Head*, by Dame Elizabeth Frink, was unveiled on South Africa Freedom Day in June 1983 to mark Nelson Mandela's 20th year of imprisonment.

A walk around the perimeter reveals numerous **plaques** bearing the names of famous former residents. Number 1, on the north side, was the childhood home of Oscar Wilde from 1855 to 1878 and is now the American College in Dublin. The 'Liberator' Daniel O'Connell lived at No 58, and W B Yeats resided at No 52 and later at No 82. Today, many of the houses serve as offices for companies and institutions. Among these are the Irish Architectural Archive, the Royal Society of Antiquaries in Ireland, and the Catholic Central Library, which houses some 60 000 books, newspapers and magazines. The **Irish Traditional Music Archive**, on the south side of the square, has a comprehensive collection of sound recordings, books and manuscripts.

Opposite the west side of the square is the green lawn of **Leinster House** (*see page 39*), with an obelisk commemorating the founders of the Irish State. Built in the mid-18th century, Leinster House is now the seat of the Irish Parliament, the Dail, and the Seanad (Senate). To the left is the **Natural History Museum** (*see page 44*), and **Government Buildings**, a neo-classical edifice built in the early 1900s which now houses the offices of the *taoiseach* (pronounced 'tea-shook'), the Irish prime minister. Tours of the lovely interior are given on Saturdays (*tel: 01 668 9333; tours given 1030–1530*). To the right is the **National Gallery** (*see page 42*).

National Botanic Gardens

Glasnevin. Tel: 01 837 7596. Open: summer, Mon–Sat 0900–1800, Sun 1100–1800; winter, Mon–Sat 1000–1630, Sun 1100–1630. £.

Cast-iron glasshouses, a palm house, a lily house and 50 acres (20 hectares) of gardens with at least 20 000 plant species are open to the public at the National Botanic Gardens in Glasnevin, in north Dublin, on the N2 road. Located on the south bank of the River Tolka, the **gardens** were founded by the Royal Dublin Society in 1795. A rose garden, rock garden, arboretum, new alpine house, weeping Atlantic cedar, large pond and area of tropical water plants and succulents provide plenty for the avid gardener to enjoy. The glasshouses, built between 1843 and 1869, and the 1884 palm house, containing tropical plants, orchids and ferns, have recently been restored.

Glasnevin's **cemetery** is famous as the last resting-place of the people who shaped Ireland – Prime Minister Eamon de Valera, Charles Stewart Parnell, Daniel O'Connell, Michael Collins and others, many of whom were executed. A free guided tour unravels the details of who did what for their country, and why (*tours leave from the main entrance on Wed and Fri at 1430*).

National Gallery

Merrion Square West. Tel: 01 661 5133. Open: Mon–Sat 1000–1730 (Thur to 2030), Sun 1400–1700. £.

The institutional 19th-century façade to the National Gallery of Ireland belies the treasure house within. Founded in 1854, the National Gallery houses an extensive collection of paintings, drawings, prints and sculpture from major European schools of painting, including works by Degas, El Greco, Goya, Monet and Picasso – to say nothing of Irish painters. One room is devoted to works by Jack B Yeats and members of his family. Some consider the *pièce de résistance* to be Vermeer's *Lady Writing a Letter*, while others vote for Caravaggio's *The Taking of Christ*, discovered in 1992 in the Dublin Jesuit House of Study.

National Library

Kildare Street. Tel: 01 603 0200. Open: Mon–Wed 1000–2100, Thur–Fri 1000–1700, Sat 1000–1300. £.

The National Library, designed by Sir Thomas Deane, opened in 1890 and houses a copy of every book ever printed in Ireland, including first editions by all the major literary figures. You can obtain a visitor's pass to see the great domed Reading Room where the likes of James Joyce and W B Yeats researched their material and no doubt gained inspiration. Exhibitions drawn from the National Museum's massive collection of books, magazines, newspapers, maps, photographs and manuscripts are mounted in the entrance hall. The library also contains the excellent **Genealogy Room**, moved here from No 2 Kildare Street, which offers advice, references and computer searches for tracing your Irish ancestry.

43

National Museum

Kildare Street. Tel: 01 677 7444. Open: Tue–Sat 1000–1700, Sun 1400–1700. £.

Opened in 1890, the magnificent building designed by Sir Thomas Deane, with its classical domed rotunda, marble pillars and zodiac mosaic floor, is a splendid storehouse for the collection of Ireland's antiquities, dating from 7 000 BC to the 20th century. The stunning gold jewellery, carved stones and iron and bronze weaponry comprises the world's largest group of Celtic artefacts. Some of the most famous pieces are kept in the **Treasury**, including the Tara Brooch, the Ardagh Chalice, St Patrick's Bell and the Cross of Cong. Exhibitions on Prehistoric Ireland, Viking Ireland and the Road to Independence put the many artefacts into historical perspective. There is also a collection of ancient Egyptian artefacts. Another branch of the National Museum, at Collins Barracks, houses the collection of decorative arts, including furniture, silver, ceramics, glassware and costume (*see page 26*).

National Wax Museum

Granby Row, Parnell Square. Tel: 01 872 6340. Open: Mon–Sat 1000–1730, Sun 1200–1730. ££.

Meet some of the people who have shaped Ireland's history at the National Wax Museum. Celebrities from the worlds of politics, literature, drama, sport, music and other fields stand before you as you listen to their biographies. There's a chamber of horrors and a captivating section for children.

Natural History Museum

Merrion Street. Tel: 01 677 7444. Open: Tue–Sat 1000–1700, Sun 1400–1700. £.

The Natural History Museum, approached from the southwestern corner of Merrion Square, is one of those splendidly old-fashioned museums with a creepy, slightly Gothic ambience. Dubliners call it 'the dead zoo', but it's informative and fun for all that. Here you'll find the skeletons of huge deer, popularly known as Irish elk, and of whales stranded on Irish beaches. There are buffalo and deer and exhibits of Irish wildlife, and jars filled with things that once wriggled, slithered or squirmed.

Newman House

Nos 85 and 86 St Stephen's Green. Tel: 01 706 7422. Open: June–Aug, Tue–Fri 1200–1700, Sat 1400–1700, Sun 1100–1400. £.

Newman House contains one of the finest Georgian interiors in the city. It is noted for its sumptuous plasterwork, particularly the late baroque Apollo Room decorated by the La Franchini brothers from Switzerland. The houses were joined in the mid-19th century when Cardinal John Newman founded the Catholic University of Ireland here. James Joyce and Flann O'Brien were former students, and the great Jesuit poet Gerard Manley Hopkins taught here towards the end of his life; the room where he lived has been restored in his honour.

Number 29

29 Fitzwilliam Street Lower. Tel: 01 702 6155. Open: Tue–Sat 1000–1700, Sun 1400–1700. £.

To see how well-heeled Dubliners lived in the late 18th and early 19th centuries, stroll round to the southeastern corner of Merrion Square and call in on the house known as Number 29. The house was restored after a public outcry at the destruction in the 1960s of 20 nearby Georgian structures to make way for a new headquarters for the Electricity Supply Board. It was furnished and decorated by the National Museum.

" *The actual course of Irish history from the late sixteenth century to the end of the eighteenth century provides abundant material for history lessons ... All you have to do is leave out the atrocities committed by your side, and provide copious details of those committed by the enemy.* "

Conor Cruise O'Brien,
***Ancestral Voices*, 1994**

Old Jameson Distillery

Bow Street, Smithfield Village. Tel: 01 807 2355. Open: daily 0930–1800 (last tour 1700). ££.

This distillery produced one of Ireland's most famous whiskeys from its beginnings in 1791 until 1966, when operations moved to County Cork. It was then turned into a museum, and now you can follow the craft of whiskey making on a guided tour. You will see the working mash tun, original copper pot stills and wooden fermentation casks, followed by a tasting in the Jameson bar.

Shaw's birthplace

33 Synge Street. Tel: 01 475 0845. Open: May–Oct, Mon–Sat 1000–1700, Sun and public holidays 1100–1700. £.

At No 1 Hatch Street Lower, which intersects about halfway down Earlsfort Terrace, the youthful George Bernard Shaw lived with his mother and her singing teacher, George Vandeleur Lee, who had invited the Shaws to stay with him. Shaw's birthplace, near by, is now a museum. The neat terraced house has been restored, looking as though the family had just stepped out for a while. Visitors can see the drawing room where Mrs Shaw held musical evenings, the parlour and the children's bedrooms. The house gives an insight into domestic life in Victorian Dublin, as well as the early years of a Nobel Prize-winning playwright.

St Patrick's Cathedral

Patrick's Close. Tel: 01 475 4817. Open: Mon–Fri 0900–1800, Sat 0900–1700 (to 1600 Nov–Feb); Sun hours: Apr–Sept, 0930–1100, 1245–1500, 1615–1700; Oct–Mar, 1000–1100, 1245–1500. ££.

Nearly 20 years younger than Christ Church Cathedral, St Patrick's stands on the oldest Christian site in Dublin. St Patrick is said to have baptised converts in a nearby well, and a church is known to have stood here since AD 450. The present edifice, the largest church in Ireland, was built in 1191, and the first **University of Ireland** was founded here in 1320. Among the highlights of the cathedral are the medieval brasses, tiles and Chapter House, the choir, with the banners and stalls of the Knights of St Patrick, and the West Tower, which dates from 1370 and contains the largest set of ringing bells in Ireland. There are also memorials to many famous people, including Carolan, the last of the Irish bards, and Douglas Hyde, the country's first president.

St Patrick's inadvertently made an unusual contribution to the English language. The phrase *'to chance your arm'* arose in 1492 when the Earl of Ormonde took refuge in the Chapter House during a feud with the Earl of Kildare. To settle the dispute, a hole was cut through the door so the two men could shake hands, without either man chancing more than an arm. You can still see the hole in the door.

Jonathan Swift served as Dean of St Patrick's from 1713 until 1745. Born of English parents in Dublin in 1667, he moved to England where he became secretary to the statesman Sir William Temple and met his lifelong companion Esther Johnson – whom he called Stella. Swift wrote many long letters to her, which were published after his death as the *Journal to Stella*. Swift and Stella now lie side by side in St Patrick's Cathedral.

In 1695 he became a minister in the Church of Ireland. As a powerful supporter of the Tory government he wrote many articles defending Tory policies – in effect, he was an early spin doctor. In recognition of his political work, Queen Anne appointed him Dean of St Patrick's Cathedral, a disappointment for him because he really wanted a church position in England. He spent the rest of his life at St Patrick's, and although he yearned for England, he switched his political energies to supporting the cause of the Irish against British abuses. He wrote *Gulliver's Travels*, *The Drapier's Letter*, *A Modest Proposal* and many satirical pamphlets. In his last years, Swift's physical and mental health declined and he died on 19 October 1745.

> *" Here He Lies, Where Savage Indignation Can No Longer Lacerate His Heart! "*
>
> **Swift's epitaph, written by himself, over his tomb in St Patrick's Cathedral**

St Stephen's Green

Dublin's largest square – a quarter of a mile in each direction and covering 27 acres (11 hectares) – St Stephen's Green is a verdant space with formal lawns, flower gardens, an ornamental lake and a Victorian bandstand. It was a tract of rough common ground until 1664 when the City Corporation set it aside as an open space for the use of citizens.

The land was ploughed, levelled, planted with trees and enclosed by a stone wall. The trouble was, no one could get there. Access from the city to the new park was along a rough lane, which was 'so foule and out of repaire that persons cannot passe'. In 1671 the Corporation ordered that the lane should be put in order, and pedestrians have been using **Grafton Street** as the main route to St Stephen's Green ever since.

During the latter part of the 18th century the north side was known as Beaux' Walk, after the aristocratic gentlemen who strolled there. Today, some of Dublin's most exclusive gentlemen's clubs are to be found in this stretch. Here, too, is the eminent **Shelbourne Hotel**, said to be 'the most distinguished address in Ireland'. The entrance alone, adorned by the figures of Nubian maidens and their slaves, to say nothing of the top-hatted doorman, marks it as one of the world's grandest hotels.

The green is dotted with monuments. The first thing you see as you leave Grafton Street is **Fusiliers' Arch**, a massive structure commemorating soldiers of the Dublin Fusiliers who served in the Anglo-Boer War. Among others, there are memorials to the writers Yeats and Joyce, the patriots Robert Emmet and Wolfe Tone, the moving Famine memorial and the bronze statue group, the *Three Fates*.

Temple Bar

Temple Bar is a place for fun. Its narrow old streets, laid out in the 18th century and now mostly pedestrianised, are a maze of bistros, boutiques, cafés, ethnic restaurants, pubs and art galleries, many of which have frontages decorated with vivid murals. It is home to a number of cultural centres, and there's always something going on – jazz and rock festivals, art exhibitions, open-air theatre.

Temple Bar lies south of the river between Grattan and O'Connell Bridges and stretches back to Dame Street. You can reach it from any side turning on the north side of Dame Street, but the best way is to cross Ha'penny Bridge from the opposite side of the Liffey and enter the district through Merchants' Arch. This gives the keenest experience of the medieval bazaar ambience that pervades Temple Bar.

Culturally, there's something for everyone. **The Ark Children's Cultural Centre** (*11A Eustace Street; tel: 01 670 7788; open: Tue–Fri 0930–1600, Sat 1000–1600; ££*) is an arts centre for children aged 4 to 14. It has a theatre, workshop and gallery. **Temple Bar Gallery and Studios** (*5–9 Temple Bar; tel: 01 671 0073; open: Mon–Sat 1000–1800, Sun 1400–1800; £*), a former factory, has been converted to provide exhibition space and working studios for 30 professional artists in all media, including painting, sculpture and photography. The best known of Temple Bar's clubs – and reputed to be the best in the city – is **Kitchen** (*East Essex Street; tel: 01 677 6635; open: daily 2330–0230; ££*), owned by the band U2. The main dance floor is surrounded by a moat!

Maze of fun

To find out what's going on in the area, call at the Temple Bar Information Centre (18 Eustace Street; tel: 01 671 5717).

Trinity College

Queen Elizabeth I founded Trinity College in 1592 because she wanted to keep higher education in Ireland firmly in Protestant hands. Roman Catholics were excluded as students until the 1970s. Today, its chapel is the only multi-denominational place of worship in the Republic. Women were admitted as students in 1903, and the total student population now numbers around 8 000. Among its most famous graduates are Jonathan Swift, Bram Stoker, Oscar Wilde and Samuel Beckett.

Front gate

Stone likenesses of two of Dublin's literary giants of the 18th century flank Trinity's main entrance. On the left, as you face the gate, is a statue of **Edmund Burke** (1729–97), the political writer who became a British Member of Parliament. On the right is **Oliver Goldsmith** (1728–74), poet and playwright. Both men studied at Trinity. The statues are the work of John Foley and were completed in the 1860s. Foley must have used the same model for the lower half of each statue – the two figures have identical legs.

Parliament Square

None of the College's original Elizabethan buildings has survived, but their loss has been amply compensated by the magnificent Palladian structures surrounding **Parliament Square**, so called because much of its cost was met by the 18th-century Irish government. If the scene seems familiar, it's probably because this was where much of the 1983 film *Educating Rita* was shot.

Parliament Square is dominated by the massive **Campanile**, donated in 1853 by the Archbishop of Armagh and designed by Sir Charles Lanyon, architect of Queen's University, Belfast. Facing each other beyond the first pair of lawns are the **Examination Hall** (on the right) and the **Chapel**, both designed by Sir William Chambers.

Trinity College Library

The lawned area behind the campanile is known as **Library Square**, and the row of red-brick buildings at the far end are the **Rubrics**, the oldest surviving buildings in the College, dating from 1700. To the right of the Rubrics is the **Old Library**, built in 1732, which contains the magnificent **Long Room**, the largest single chamber library in Europe, measuring 213ft (65m) in length and housing some 200 000 volumes on high wooden shelves.

On the ground floor, The Colonnades exhibition gallery displays the world-famous *Book of Kells*, thought to have been produced by the monks of Iona in the early 9th century. An excellent exhibition, *Turning Darkness into Light*, introduces this treasure and provides a fascinating look at how these lavishly decorated gospels were produced.

Beyond Library Square are Trinity's newer developments, including New Square (1838–44) and the Berkeley Library Building (1967). The Thomas Davis Theatre houses the audio-visual presentation, the *Dublin Experience*.

Getting there: Trinity College Library. Tel: 01 608 2320. Open: Mon–Sat 0930–1700; Sun, Oct–May 1200–1630, June–Sept 0930–1630. ££. Try to visit Trinity College Library early in the day, when it is less crowded with tour bus groups.

Eating and drinking

Ayumi-Ya
132 Lower Baggot Street. Tel: 01 662 0233. £. Informal, inexpensive eating in Ireland's first Japanese restaurant established in 1983.

Beshoff's Restaurant
Lower O'Connell Street. £. Long-established restaurant serving the best fish and chips in Dublin.

Botticelli
3 Temple Bar. Tel: 01 672 7289. ££. Some Dubliners say this is the best place for authentic Italian pasta and pizzas. Reservations essential.

Burdock's
2 Werburgh Street. Tel: 01 454 0306. Open: Mon–Fri 1230–midnight, Sat 1400–2300, Sun 1600–midnight. £. A Dublin institution – the city's oldest fish and chip shop. Strictly take-away fresh fish with chips made from Irish potatoes. No place for vegetarians, though – the exquisite chips are fried in beef dripping.

Cooke's Café
14 William Street South. Tel: 01 679 0536. ££. New age Mediterranean, Californian and seafood dishes.

Dobbins
15 Stephen's Lane. Tel: 01 676 4679. ££. A favourite with Dublin journalists and politicians, this is a fun eating place with a welcoming and attentive staff, led by their congenial boss, John O'Byrne.

Dyflin
Bedford Row, Temple Bar. Tel: 01 677 8528. £–££. Large windows looking out on the passing scene at Temple Bar. The menu ranges from hot chicken and vegetable salads, to pastas and pizzas, to lamb, chicken and pork dishes.

Fitzers
51 Dawson Street. Tel: 01 677 1155. £–££. Enjoy the outdoor tables beneath a big blue awning or the smart dining room with modern prints on the walls. Light bistro-style menu with Pacific influences.

Gallagher's Boxty House
20–21 Temple Bar. Tel: 01 677 2762. ££. Boxty is a potato pancake stuffed with marinated beef, chicken or other fillings. Book or come early to this popular restaurant.

Il Posto
10 St Stephen's Green. Tel: 01 679 4769. ££. Authentic Italian cuisine in simple but comfortable surroundings.

La Cave
28 Anne Street South. Tel: 01 679 4409. £–££. Carnivores and vegetarians can both find satisfaction in the city's oldest French wine bar.

Le Caprice
12 St Andrew Street. Tel: 01 679 4050. Open: Tue–Sat 1800–0015. £££. A pianist plays as diners enjoy what many regard as the finest Italian fare in Dublin. Dublin Bay provides fresh supplies of seafood daily.

Lord Edward
23 Christchurch Place. Tel: 01 454 2420. Open for lunch Mon–Fri, dinner Mon–Sat. ££–£££. The city's oldest seafood restaurant (circa 1968) offers dishes that reflect its experience. Lunch is served in the ground floor pub, dinner in the upstairs restaurant.

Mermaid Café

60–70 Dame Street. Tel: 01 670 8236. Open: for lunch and dinner Mon–Sat, brunch and dinner (to 2130) Sun. £–££. Imaginative cuisine from Ben Gorman, one of Ireland's leading chefs. Reasonably priced and served in light and airy surroundings.

Peacock Alley

47 William Street South. Tel: 01 662 0760. ££–£££. Mediterranean food served with panache by an Irish chef whose talent was honed in the competitive kitchens of New York. Conrad Gallagher's restaurant is the city's most prestigious.

Restaurant Patrick Guilbaud

21 Upper Merrion Street. Tel: 01 676 4192. Open for lunch and dinner Tue–Sat. £££. Dubliners know it simply as 'RPG', where the best of Irish produce becomes the best of French cuisine.

Pubs

A genial insight into Dublin's literature, history and architecture is provided on the **Jameson Dublin Literary Pub Crawl** (*tel: 01 454 0228*). The tours are led by actors who play some of the city's most colourful characters as groups progress from pub to pub, starting at **The Duke** (*9 Duke Street*), a pub that has the careworn charm of an old tweed jacket and is the haunt of cheerful but slightly world-weary bar-room philosophers and wannabe writers. You can tune in to some great conversations here.

Across the street from Dublin's tourist information centre is **O'Neill's** (*2 Suffolk Street*), an atmospheric old Dublin pub with the best carvery in the city, serving from noon to 1430. It's bigger than it looks from the outside and is full of nooks and crannies. Be warned, however: it is a favourite lunch spot with the city's workers, so get there by 1230 or after 1400 or you won't find a seat.

Another popular pub in the area is **The Old Stand** (*37 Exchequer Street*), very traditional with lots of dark mahogany. The food's traditional, too: Irish stew, bacon and cabbage, and its steaks are legendary.

There's no shortage of watering holes in the Grafton Street vicinity. **The Bailey** (*2 Duke Street*) was a favourite with James Joyce, Brendan Behan and Patrick Kavanagh. **Davy Byrne's**, across the street at No 21, features in Joyce's *Ulysses* and has a restaurant renowned for its seafood and traditional Irish dishes. The discrete old snugs at **Keyhoe's** (*9 South Anne Street*) make eavesdropping difficult. **McDaid's** (*3 Harry Street*) is the quintessential Dublin pub.

Doheny and Nesbitt (*5 Lower Baggot Street; tel: 01 676 2945*) sounds more like a firm of solicitors than a pub, and in fact many of its clients are lawyers, but it's a jolly place for all that, and a Dublin classic. **O'Donoghue's** (*15 Merrion Row; tel: 01 660 7194*) has a reputation for putting on good Irish music that began with The Dubliners and continues with today's up-and-coming performers.

The Brazen Head (*20 Bridge Street Lower; tel: 01 677 9549*) is Dublin's oldest pub (built in the 1660s but standing on the site of an inn that first opened in 1198). As you would expect, there is lots of atmosphere, with stone walls, open fires, traditional music and sing-along sessions.

Shopping

*O'Connell Street has a good mix of shops. The main department store is **Clery's**, which has a craft shop. **Eason and Sons'** spacious bookshop has a large section devoted to just about every aspect of Ireland.*

Works of art can be bought at galleries either side of the Liffey in the vicinity of the Ha'penny Bridge, where there is a variety of antique and collectables shops and other specialist stores. The **Dublin Woollen Mills** shop is enticing, with traditional Irish knitwear and expensive sports jackets. Outside it is a modern sculpture of two women shoppers, affectionately called 'the hags with the bags' by Dubliners.

Even if you don't play an instrument, you'll find a fascinating range of Irish harps, pipes, flutes, fiddles, accordions and bodhráns – small goatskin drums – at **Walton's** in North Frederick Street, which has been trading for more than 75 years. There are CDs and cassettes of Irish music.

McDowell's, in Upper O'Connell Street, sells gold and silver hand-crafted souvenir jewellery and Waterford crystal.

Pedestrianised Grafton Street itself has an eclectic range of shops and is a great place for drifting and window-shopping without the need for traffic-dodging. The leading department stores here are **Brown Thomas**, up-market without being stand-offish, and neighbouring **Marks & Spencer**, the British shopping institution.

Jewellery shops are dotted all over the area. Start your search in Johnson's Court, alongside Bewley's. Here you'll find something for all tastes and budgets. And for those who don't have to think about a budget, there's **Appleby's**. Modern Irish creations are on display – and on sale – at the **Crafts Council of Ireland** section of the Powerscourt Townhouse Centre.

Craft shops also abound. **The House of Ireland**, on Nassau Street, between Grafton and Dawson streets, sells top quality items in crystal, leather, linen, porcelain and wool. **Blarney Woollen Mills**, on the corner of Nassau Street and Frederick Street South, is the place in this part of town for hand-woven garments and traditional knitwear. For Irish linen goods make your way to **Needlecraft**, 27 Dawson Street, where you will also find everything you need to engage in knitting, crochet or embroidery.

Music-lovers are well served. **HMV** has a three-storey record emporium and ticket agency at 65 Grafton Street, while the ubiquitous **Tower Records**, complete with a special section selling books and magazines, can be found at 16 Wicklow Street. **Golden Discs**, Ireland's largest chain of music stores, has a branch on Grafton Street, next to the Grafton Arcade. **Celtic Note**, 12 Nassau Street, specialises in Irish music. If you're looking for second-hand bargains on cassette or disc, seek out **Borderline**, Duke's Lane.

Nightlife

For arts and entertainment listings *The Irish Times* and *The Evening Herald* have guides to theatres, cinemas, live music and other events. *In Dublin* and *The Event Guide* are two free fortnightly guides distributed in pubs and cafés around town; they also have dance club listings.

There are numerous nightclubs in the city centre, with some of the trendiest located on the quays on the north side of the Liffey. Two of the best places to hear traditional music are south of the city centre. **Johnnie Fox's** (*tel: 01 295 5647*) is a characterful pub at Glencullen, in the Dublin mountains off the Enniskerry road. **Comhaltas Ceoltóirí Éireann**, the association for the promotion of traditional music and culture, has its headquarters in Belgrave Square, Monkstown, where it organises nightly entertainment from June to September. It also holds a Céili on Friday nights year round (*tel: 01 280 0295 for information*).

Da Club
2 Johnson's Place, off Clarendon Row. Tel: 01 670 5116. Open: Mon–Sat 2230–0200. 'Da' is short for Dublin Arts. Stand-up comedy, live music and witty DJs.

Gaiety Theatre
King Street South. Tel: 01 677 1717. Open: Fri–Sat 2300–0230. Cabaret, jazz and rock groups keep the action going in three bars, and there's a disco, too.

PoD
Corner of Hatch Street, Harcourt Street. Tel: 01 478 0225. Open: Wed– Sun 2300–0230. The city's stylish 'Place of Dance'. Upstairs is the noisier, more adolescent **Red Box** (*open: Thur–Sat 2200–0230*).

The arts

The **Abbey** (*tel: 01 878 7222*) and its sister, the **Peacock**, are the two theatres of the National Theatre Society, founded by W B Yeats, Lady Gregory and J M Synge. Since its birth, the Society has premièred the work of every leading Irish playwright, and continues to promote new writing and acting talent in its productions today. The **Gate Theatre** (*tel: 01 874 4045*) produces classics and contemporary Irish plays. Opera, musical comedy and revues are staged at the **Gaiety Theatre** (*tel: 01 677 1717*), while the **Olympia Theatre** (*tel: 01 677 7744*) puts on vaudeville, comedy and ballet, as well as music productions every Friday and Saturday night from midnight.

The **National Concert Hall** (*tel: 01 475 1666*) is the main venue for classical music performances. Concerts are also held at the **Royal Hospital Kilmainham** (*tel: 01 671 8666*).

Cafés

The ground floor of **Bewley's Café**, on Grafton Street, is where Dubliners of all ages meet to enjoy a bit of character assassination over tea and cream cakes. It's quieter upstairs among the potted palms. If you don't want to queue for coffee here, try the **Metro Café**, off the beaten Grafton Street track on South William Street. This mellow café is a popular hang-out for young Dubliners and serves great cappuccino. There are also a couple of cafés on Anne Street, such as the trendy **Gotham**.

The difference an 'e' makes

Only an 'e' marks the difference in spelling, but purists will tell you that the two products are as different as chalk and cheese. We're talking alcohol, of course. Whiskey in Ireland – without the 'e' in Scotland. Both are made from barley and are the result of distillation. Beyond that point, Scottish and Irish distillers part company.

The characteristic smoky flavour of Scotch comes from the open peat fires over which the malted barley is dried. The Irish, surprisingly, considering how much peat they have and burn, dry their barley in smoke-free, coke-fired kilns. The result is a clear, clean barley taste.

The Irish also point out that their whiskey is distilled three times, while most similar spirits produced in Scotland and elsewhere are distilled only twice. They also claim their product came first.

Distillation was first practised in the Middle East, long before the birth of Christ. Aristotle mentioned the process in the 4th century BC, but in the beginning it was used solely for making perfume.

'Water of life'

The Irish put the art to better use when distillation was introduced to them by Christian missionaries around AD 600. They made a product for internal consumption only and named it *Uisce Beatha* (pronounced 'Ishkay Ba-ha'), meaning 'the water of life'. The phrase was too difficult for English soldiers serving in Ireland in the 12th century – even after drinking the stuff – so they shortened the name to 'whiskey'.

Potheen

At one time the Irish landscape was dotted with distilleries – more than 2 000 were known to be in operation – but today there are only two (to say nothing of a few moonshiners making *potheen* in quiet country corners). Between them, the distilleries at Midleton, Co Cork, and Bushmills, Co Antrim (*see page 204*), make the full range of individual whiskeys which are as distinctive in taste as the labels on their bottles.

Despite their reputation, the Irish, it seems, are not a nation of drinkers. Official statistics claim that 50 per cent of the population is teetotal. 'But the other half more than make up for them,' says a Dublin tour guide.

Around Dublin

From the Dublin suburbs, Ireland's wild green landscape opens out to reveal idyllic houses and gardens, historic battle sites, prehistoric mounds and the high crosses of early Irish monasticism.

Around Dublin

Getting there: sights close to Dublin can be reached by using the DART railway, which goes north as far as Howth and south to Bray and Greystones. Feeder bus services link with the DART system to take you on to towns and popular visitor attractions in the Dublin area. Even so, you will find that driving offers the easiest way of getting around.

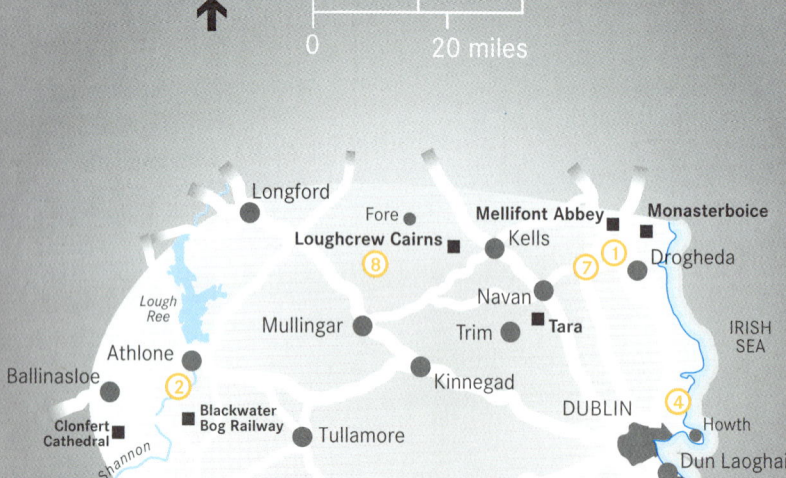

North

0   50 km

0   20 miles

Longford

Fore
Loughcrew Cairns   ⑧   Kells   **Mellifont Abbey**   **Monasterboice**

⑦   ①   Drogheda

Lough Ree   Mullingar   Navan   **Tara**

IRISH SEA

Ballinasloe   Athlone   ②   Trim

Kinnegad

Clonfert Cathedral   **Blackwater Bog Railway**   DUBLIN   ④   Howth

R. Shannon   Tullamore   Dun Laoghai

Dalkey

Birr   ③   ⑥   ⑤   Bray

① *Brú Na Bóinne (Newgrange)*

Penetrate the dark central chamber of this massive and awe-inspiring Neolithic tumulus and wonder what rituals went on here some 5 000 years ago to honour the dead. See if you can guess the meaning of the strange geometric patterns inscribed on the massive stones lining the passage to the tomb. **Pages 64–5**

② *Clonmacnoise*

Visit the extensive remains of one of Ireland's most important monastic sites, flourishing and producing great art when the rest of Europe was being harried by barbarians. **Page 66**

③ *Kildare*

Even if you're not a race-goer, you'll enjoy the sheer animal beauty of the thoroughbreds at the National Stud, not to mention the peaceful and richly planted Japanese Gardens alongside. **Pages 70–1**

④ *Malahide Castle*

There is something to please everyone at Malahide Castle, from beautiful period furnishings and a collection of portraits from the National Gallery to the Talbot Botanic Gardens and the Fry Model Railway. **Page 72**

⑤ *Powerscourt House and Gardens*

Ireland's finest gardens await your visit, laid out in the theatrical Italian style with gushing fountains, statues of Roman deities, terraced stairways and charmingly naturalistic woodland. **Page 75**

⑥ *Russborough House*

A fortune was lavished on creating luxurious Russborough House, with its grand Italianate interiors and art collection, including works by Rubens, Reynolds, Gainsborough, Murillo and Guardi. **Page 76**

⑦ *Slane Hill*

St Patrick lit a fire here in AD 433 in defiance of local Druidic practice, and the rest is history. The atmospheric place offers panoramic views over the site of the Battle of the Boyne. **Page 77**

⑧ *Tullynally Castle*

Gothic and splendid, this castle offers an insight into life below stairs, with its extensive Victorian kitchens and laundries. The grounds include walled gardens, grottoes and ornamental lakes. **Page 79**

Athlone

Tourist Information Office: Athlone Castle. Tel: 0902 94630. Open: Apr–Oct.

Athlone lies 77 miles (124km) west of Dublin, a comfortable two-hour drive along the N4 and N6. It's a busy town, whose main attraction – apart from its shops – is 13th-century **Athlone Castle** (*Market Square; tel: 0902 72107; open: May–Sept daily 1000–1700; £*). The castle offers a good introduction to the region, with exhibitions and audio-visual presentations on local flora and fauna, and the 1691 Siege of Athlone that followed the Battle of the Boyne. A special presentation features the life of the celebrated tenor, Count John McCormack, who was born in the town.

The town is also a base for pleasure cruises on the River Shannon and Lough Ree. The **MV *Ross*** takes passengers on a 90-minute cruise (*£££*) from the Jolly Mariner Marina (*tel: 0902 72892; open: daily Apr–Sept*). **Rossana Cruises** (*tel: 0902 73383*) has trips along the Shannon to Clonmacnoise and entertaining cruises to Lough Ree, with tales of Viking warbands and treasure islands.

Birr

Tourist Information Office: tel: 0509 20110. Open: May–Sept.

Birr is a splendid example of a small-scale Georgian town. Its spacious, tree-lined avenues, with their handsome squares and houses, date from the 1740s. Oxmantown Mall and John's Mall are especially fine, with graceful façades sporting

fanlights, panelled doors and other classic Georgian features. The town is a walker's delight with myriad charming corners, from the traditional shopfronts on Connaught Street and Mercy Convent designed by Pugin, to the riverside walk along the south bank of the Camcor.

The main attraction today is **Birr Castle Demesne** (*tel: 0509 20336; open: Apr–Oct, daily 0900–1800; Nov–Mar daily, 0900–1300, 1400–dusk; £*), home of the earls of Rosse. The early 18th-century castle is not open to the public, but the surrounding 100 acres (25 hectares) of grounds are, and really should not be missed. The formal gardens, based on a 17th-century layout, include the world's tallest box hedges, recorded in the *Guinness Book of Records* at a height of 32ft (9m), plus thousands of trees and shrubs, many very rare, from all parts of the world. The coach house is used to house galleries of Ireland's Historic Science Centre, with information on the Great Telescope, a 72-inch reflecting telescope built by the 3rd earl in the 1840s and the largest in the world at the time. It still operates, and demonstrations are given daily.

Blackwater Bog Railway

Shannonbridge. Tel: 0905 74114. Open: late Mar–Oct, daily 1000–1700; tours on the hour. ££.

The Clonmacnoise and West Offaly narrow-gauge railway runs through several miles of raised bog on track used by Bord na Mona (the Irish Peat Board) to harvest peat for Shannonbridge Power Station, the largest of Ireland's five peat-burning power stations. The guide explains the formation of the bogs, the traditional and commercial peat-harvesting process, the flora and fauna and the environmental reclamation of the exhausted peatlands; you can even try your hand at cutting turf. The tour lasts 45 minutes.

Bray

Tourist Information Office: tel: 01 286 7128 or 6796; fax: 01 286 0930.

At the southern limit of the DART, 14 miles (22.5km) from Dublin, Bray has more than a mile of sand and shingle beach. On warm summer days crowds flock along the esplanade and into the amusement arcades. The **National Sea-Life Centre** (*Strand Road; tel: 01 286 6939; open: Mar–Sept, 1000–1700; ring for winter hours; ££*) presents a fascinating array of marine life.

From the end of the boardwalk, a path carries on around the eastern flank of Bray Head to the fishing village of **Greystones**, about 3 miles (5km) away. There are also splendid views from the Eagle's Nest pathway leading to the top of Bray Head, which rises 791ft (241m) high. Near by, the French-style **Killruddery Gardens** (*south end of Bray, just off the Bray–Greystones road; tel: 01 286 3405; gardens open Apr–Sept daily 1300–1700; house open May, June and Sept daily 1300–1700; ££*) with twin canals and high beech hedges, were laid out in the 17th century and are a rare survivor of early, large-scale formal landscaping. About 2 miles (3km) southwest of Bray is **Powerscourt House and Gardens** estate (*see page 75*).

Brú Na Bóinne (Newgrange)

Donore. Tel: 041 988 0300. Newgrange open year-round; Knowth Mar–Apr and Oct, 0930–1700; May and mid-Sept–end Sept 0900–1830; June–mid-Sept 0900–1900; Nov–Feb 0930–1700. ££–£££.

Brú na Bóinne, the 'dwelling place of the Boyne', lies an hour's drive north of Dublin, flanking the N51 between Navan and Drogheda. The area embraces 50 of the world's most important archaeological sites. They can only be visited on a guided tour from the Newgrange visitor centre, where there are excellent exhibits and a film about the site.

Built by Neolithic farmers more than 5 000 years ago and pre-dating the Egyptian pyramids, the **Newgrange** passage grave is awe-inspiring. The mound covering the tomb is constructed of 200 000 tons of earth and water-rolled pebbles and rises to a height of 35ft (12m). Massive stones line the passage and strange geometrical symbols and spirals are inscribed on the rock. A narrow slit in the roof of the structure allows a shaft of sunlight to penetrate the inner chamber at dawn on the day of the winter solstice, a moment of great ritual significance to the Neolithic builders.

Entrance to the **Knowth** site, a mile (1.5km) from Newgrange, is restricted because of continuing archaeological activity, but several of its 17 satellite tombs may be visited. Knowth is outstanding for its rich display of megalithic art; over 300 decorated stones are contained in the main mound alone. Victorian treasure hunters plundered **Dowth's** passage grave, 2 miles (3km) from Newgrange, and the site is not open to the public, though it can be seen from the road.

Castletown House

Cellbridge. Tel: 01 628 8252. Open: Apr–Sept, daily 1000–1700; Oct, closed Mon, Nov–Mar, open Sun only. ££.

This magnificent house, built in 1722 for the Speaker of the Irish parliament, would not look out of place in the Venetian countryside, modelled as it is on the villa architecture of Andrea Palladio. The wall paintings were inspired by those of Rafael in the Vatican, and Pompeian-style friezes frame copies of ancient Greek and Roman statuary.

Clonfert Cathedral

Clonfert. Unrestricted access. £.

Fans of Romanesque architecture should seek out this tiny but richly carved church, sitting on the site of a monastery founded by St Brendan in AD 563. The east doorway is decorated with human and animal heads in niches, and later builders picked up this theme in the mermaids and angels adorning the 15th-century chancel arch.

Clonmacnoise

Near Shannonbridge. Tel: 0905 74195. Open: mid-Mar–May and mid-Sept–Oct, daily 1000–1800; June–early Sept, daily 0900–1900; Nov–mid-Mar, daily 1000–1700; closed 25 Dec. ££.

Clonmacnoise, 12 miles (19km) south of Athlone, is one of Ireland's most impressive early Christian monastic sites. Founded by St Ciaran in AD 545, Clonmacnoise became a great centre of Irish art and literature, producing the first known manuscript in the Irish language. The work of its craftsmen in precious metals was unsurpassed, though it is best known for its magnificent stone-carved high crosses, the **Cross of the Scriptures** and the **South Cross**. These have been moved inside the visitor centre to protect their intricate carvings from weathering, and replicas stand on the site.

The excellent visitor centre, housed in three buildings modelled on the beehive-shaped huts used by early monks, has a good audio-visual programme on the history of the monastery, and exhibits about the high crosses and decorated stone slabs.

Dalkey

This picturesque fishing village, home to the likes of Damon Hill, Chris de Burgh and Bono, makes a pleasant excursion by DART from Dublin. It has narrow winding streets lined with shopfronts and several good pubs and restaurants (*see page 80*). In summer a boat ferries passengers from Coliemore Harbour to the **Dalkey Island** bird sanctuary, 15 minutes away.

Dun Laoghaire

Dun Laoghaire (pronounced 'Dun Leary') is a busy seaport for freight and passenger ferries. There are two piers, each 1^1/$_2$ miles (2.5km) long: you may strike lucky and be serenaded by one of the bands that sometimes play here on a summer's day. Housed in the former 1830s Mariners' Church, the **National Maritime Museum** unfolds some interesting stories (*Haigh Terrace; tel: 01 280 0968; open: May–Sept, Tue–Sun 1430–1730; £*). In the early 1900s James Joyce spent a week as a guest in the Martello tower at nearby **Sandycove**. Later, he used the tower as the setting for the first chapter of *Ulysses*. The tower now contains a delightful little museum displaying Joyce first editions, photographs, letters and personal possessions (*tel: 01 280 9265; open: Apr–Oct, Mon–Sat 1000–1700, Sun and public holidays 1400–1800; £*).

Drogheda

Tourist Information Office: Bus Éireann station, N1 and Donore Road. Tel: 041 983 7070; fax: 041 984 5340. Open: all year.

Set on the banks of the River Boyne, its skyline punctuated by the spires of three cathedrals, Drogheda is one of the most attractive medieval towns in the Irish Midlands. By the early 15th century the walled and fortified town was the largest English town in the country. Cromwell launched a savage attack on Drogheda in 1649, and **St Lawrence Gate** is the only sizeable remnant – and a handsome one – of the medieval defences. On West Street, the Gothic Catholic **Church of St Peter** houses a sad and rather gruesome relic: the head of the martyred saint, Oliver Plunkett. Born of a prominent Meath family, he became the Archbishop of Armagh, but was falsely convicted of instigating a 'Popish Plot' and was hung, drawn and quartered in 1681. The mummified head is visibly displayed in a side chapel. The **Millmount Museum** (*tel: 041 983 3097; open: Mon–Sat 1000–1700, Sun 1430–1700; £*) on the outskirts of town has a wonderful collection of guild parade banners.

Fore

Nestling in a beautiful green valley, this tiny village keeps watch over some of Ireland's most atmospheric monastic ruins. As you approach, the remains of 13th-century **Fore Abbey** (*open daily, unrestricted access*) the country's largest Benedictine site, glisten in the surrounding bog. On the hill opposite the abbey are the remains of **St Feichin's Church**. Legend claims the massive lintel was raised in place by the saint's prayers, one of the 'seven wonders' associated with the site. The medieval stone gateways still stand at either end of the village.

Howth

This attractive harbour town lies on Dublin Bay, about half an hour from the city by DART. The steep winding streets of the village have good restaurants and pubs (*see page 81*), and there are several enjoyable walks here, the easiest leading out along the sea wall, with fine views of the boats in the harbour and the rock island offshore known as 'Ireland's Eye'. Local boatmen can take you there in good weather to see the old stone church and Martello tower. A 1½-mile (2.5km) cliff walk takes you around the headland to the Baily Lighthouse, where there are splendid views. You can visit the grounds of **Howth Castle** (*tel: 01 832 2624; open: daily 0800–dusk; £*), which have beautiful rhododendron gardens, a ruined 16th-century castle and a Neolithic dolmen. The **National Transport Museum** is also located in the grounds (*tel: 01 848 0831; open: Easter–Sept, daily 1000–1730; Oct–Easter, weekends and public holidays 1400–1730; ££*). The exhibits include horse-drawn commercial vehicles, carriages, fire-fighting appliances, early motor vehicles and the open-top Hill of Howth tram.

Kells

Kells, or Ceanannus Mór, is famed for the monastery founded by St Colmcille in the 6th century. Monks from the island of Iona fled here in the 9th century. They were the creators of the magnificent *Book of Kells*, which can be seen at Trinity College in Dublin (*see page 51*) – a copy of the book is displayed here in St Columba's Church, where the gallery has other exhibits relating to the monastery. A 100ft- (30.5m-) high round tower stands in the graveyard of the church. The scriptural high cross of Saints Patrick and Columba is the finest of four carved crosses.

Kildare

Tourist Information Office: tel: 045 522696. Open: June–mid-Sept.

Kildare's 13th-century **Cathedral** (*The Square; tel: 045 521229; open: Mon–Sat 1000–1300, 1400–1700, Sun 1400–1700; £*) stands on the site where St Brigid founded a community of monks and nuns in the 5th century. In the graveyard is a **Round Tower**, believed to be from the 12th century. At 108ft (33m), it is one of the highest in Ireland.

Kildare's people live and breathe racing, and most of its visitors are not tourists but race-goers. The Curragh, Ireland's famous flat-racing venue, is 4 miles (6.5km) to the east. The **National Stud** (*tel: 045 21617; open: mid-Feb–mid-Nov, daily 0930–1800; £££*), just outside the town at Tully, covers 958 acres (390 hectares). Colonel William Hall-Walker, a Scotsman, began breeding thoroughbred horses here in 1900. A great believer in astrology, he built skylights into his stables so that the heavens could exert their maximum influence on his horses. With nearly 300 horseboxes, its own saddlery and forge, the National Stud now occupies around 1 000 acres (405 hectares). Stallions with gleaming coats and rippling muscles graze in paddocks alongside the Oak Walk. The Tully Walk passes by paddocks where mares and foals live when the breeding season is over. A museum outlines the history of the horse and its importance in Ireland. A new visitor centre has a craft shop, restaurant and children's Lego area.

Sharing the same estate as the Irish National Stud are the Japanese Gardens. Devised by Hall-Walker, they were laid out by a Japanese gardener, Tassa Eida, and his son, Minoru, between 1906 and 1910. The gardens symbolically depict the soul's journey through life, passing through the Hill of Learning to the Well of Wisdom.

Loughcrew Cairns

Near Oldcastle. Tel: 049 854 2009. Cairn T open: mid-June–mid-Sept, daily 1000–1800; site accessible all year. ££.

Ireland's largest Stone Age necropolis is spread across three peaks of the Slieve-na-Caillighe, or Loughcrew Hills. Some 30 chambered cairns dating between 2500 and 3000 BC have been excavated here, making it one of the most important archaeological sites in the country. On the days of the spring and autumn equinox, sunlight enters the tomb at dawn and illuminates a series of patterns on the stones inside. Such orientation and symbolic carvings emphasises the ritual nature of the site. The views of the surrounding countryside are magnificent.

Malahide Castle

Tel: 01 846 2184. Open: Apr–Oct, Mon–Sat 1000–1700, Sun 1100–1800; Nov–Mar, Mon–Fri 1000–1700, Sat–Sun 1400–1700; closed for tours from 1245–1400. ££.

Set in parkland in the seaside town of Malahide, the castle makes a good day-trip from the city. The fortress, built in 1185, was the home of the Talbot family for nearly 800 years. Its mix of architectural styles includes the medieval Great Hall, the Tudor Oak Room, and rococo plasterwork in the reception rooms. It contains beautiful period furnishings and a collection of portraits from the National Gallery.

The castle has 250 acres (100 hectares) of grounds, including the **Talbot Botanic Gardens** (*tel: 01 846 2456; open: May–Sept, daily 1400–1700*), whose 5 000 labelled species represent Ireland's largest collection of southern hemisphere plants.

Also in the grounds is the **Fry Model Railway Museum** (*tel: 01 846 3779, fax: 01 846 2537; open: Apr–Sept, Mon–Thur 1000–1800, Sat 1100– 1800, Sun and public holidays 1400–1800, closed Fri, June–Aug, Fri 1000–1800, Oct–Mar, Sat, Sun and public holidays 1100–1700; £*), a charming arrangement of miniature trains, railway stations, bridges, trams, buses, the River Liffey, river craft and recognisable Dublin landmarks. The Irish and foreign locomotives and trains are superbly crafted models from the early days of the railways to more recent times. The collection began over 70 years ago, when a railway engineer and draughtsman, Cyril Fry, meticulously produced each model in detail

Mellifont Abbey

Tel: 041 26459. Open: May–mid-June and mid-Sept–Oct, daily 1000–1700; mid-June–mid-Sept, daily 0930–1830. ££.

Founded by St Malachy in 1142, Mellifont Abbey was the first Cistercian monastery in Ireland. It marked the introduction of the European monastic system in a country where independent, less hierarchical monastic settlements were the rule. When it was dissolved in 1539, Mellifont ranked as the second wealthiest Cistercian house in the country (after St Mary's Abbey in Dublin). The property

was subsequently converted into a fortified house, and during the Battle of the Boyne William of Orange made his headquarters here. Mellifont's ruins are more fragmentary than other sites. Its finest feature is the octagonal Romanesque *lavabo*, where the monks washed before entering the refectory, built in the early 13th century. There is a small architectural museum on the site.

Monasterboice

Site accessible daily, all year round.

Founded in the 6th century by St Buite, Monasterboice was a renowned centre of learning in the 11th century, but it fell into decline with the establishment of nearby Mellifont Abbey. Two of Ireland's finest high crosses stand in the cemetery amid the ruins of the monastery. **Muiredach's Cross**, named after the 10th-century abbot for whom it was made, stands over 17ft (5m) high; the shaft and head were carved from a single block of sandstone. The scriptural carvings are outstanding for the details of dress, accoutrement and gesture, and depict such scenes as Cain killing Abel and David slaying Goliath. The **West Cross**, at 23ft (7m) high, is the tallest in Ireland. It has a unique carving of Jesus walking on the water and saving Peter from drowning. The third, less notable **North Cross** was also carved in the 10th century. The **Round Tower**, minus its top, once held a great monastic library and other treasures, which were destroyed in a fire in 1097.

Mullingar

Tourist Information Office: Dublin Road. Tel: 044 48650.

The twin spires of the Renaissance-style **Cathedral of Christ the King** dominate Mullingar's skyline (*open: daily 0900–1730; ecclesiastical museum open: Thur, Sat and Sun 1600–1700, or contact the sacristan; tel: 044 48402*). Inside are superb mosaics of St Patrick and St Anne by the Russian artist Boris Anrep, and an ecclesiastical museum. Mullingar is a former garrison town, and artefacts from the various conflicts in Irish history are displayed in the **Military Museum** (*Columb Barracks; tel: 044 48391; open: by appointment only*). There is an energetic, friendly feel to this market town, which has become a popular touring base for the region. Mullingar is also at the heart of Ireland's cattle-raising lands, and farmers across the country judge a good cow as 'beef to the heels, like a Mullingar heifer'.

Powerscourt House and Gardens

Enniskerry. Tel: 01 204 6000. Open: Mar–Oct, daily 0930–1730. ££.

Powerscourt, one of the finest estates in Ireland, takes its name from the Le Poer (Power) family, who built a castle here in 1300. In 1603, the lands were granted to the Englishman Richard Wingfield, whose descendants remained for over 350 years. Between 1731 and 1740, Richard Castle, the architect of Russborough House, converted the castle into an impressive Palladian mansion, which once boasted the grandest ballroom in the country. However, a tragic fire in 1974 gutted the building, and all that stands inside the massive shell are some ground-floor shops, a terrace café and an exhibition that describes its former glory. There are long-term plans to restore the ballroom.

The magnificent **Powerscourt Gardens** are the real attraction. A monumental terrace sweeps down to the lake, where graceful winged horses frame the **Triton fountain**, spurting a high stream against the backdrop of the Great Sugar Loaf Mountain. Much of the credit goes to the landscape architect Daniel Robertson, who drew up garden designs for the 6th Viscount Powerscourt in the 1840s and directed the work from a wheelbarrow, staving off his gout pains with a bottle of sherry. Later generations continued to enhance the grounds, and today the 47-acre (19-hectare) demesne is adorned with leafy avenues, specimen trees, ponds, fine statuary and ironwork, a pepper-pot tower and Italianate, Japanese and walled gardens.

Four miles (6km) away, accessible on foot from the gardens, is the magnificent River Dargle **waterfall**, with a drop of more than 300ft (100m).

Russsborough House

2 miles (3km) south of Blessington, off the N81. Tel: 045 865239. Open: Apr and Oct, Sun and public holidays 1030–1730; May and Sept, Mon–Sat 1030–1430, Sun 1030–1730; June–Aug, daily 1030–1730; closed Nov–Easter. ££.

In 1741 Joseph Leeson, later the Earl of Milltown, decided to spend his newly acquired fortune on building one of the finest Palladian-style mansions in the country. Russsborough House was designed by Richard Castle, the architect of Powerscourt House, and finished by Francis Bindon after Castle's death. The palatial façade, built of silver Wicklow granite and flanked by semicircular loggias and wings, conceals a baroque interior with elaborate plasterwork ceilings. Sir Alfred Beit purchased Russsborough in 1952 and for a time it was the home of one of Europe's finest private art collections. After two major robberies, many of the paintings were donated to the National Gallery of Ireland. Works by Rubens, Reynolds, Gainsborough, Murillo and Guardi still remain, along with displays of fine porcelain, silver and bronzes. Visitors can also wander among the extensive woodlands.

Slane Hill

According to tradition, Slane Hill, about 7 miles (11km) northeast of Navan (signposted off the N2), is where St Patrick first preached the Christian message to the Irish, lighting the first paschal fire on Easter Sunday, AD 433. In doing so, he unknowingly disobeyed King Laoghaire of nearby Tara, for this was a night when, according to the Druidic religion, no fires could be lit. When Patrick's fire was seen, one of the Druid leaders prophesied that if the flames were not quenched now they would burn forever and consume Tara – which, figuratively, they did. The Easter fire is still lit here each year. The remains of **Slane Abbey** stand on the site of a 5th-century monastery, a short walk across the field from the statue of St Patrick. There are panoramic views over the Boyne Valley, site of the Battle of the Boyne, which saw the defeat of the Catholic James II of England by William of Orange on 1 July 1690.

Tara

The Hill of Tara lies 8 miles (13km) south of Navan, near the village of Kilmessan. The site itself, which consists of grassy mounds, wide ditches and earthworks, is freely accessible daily year-round, but there is a charge for entering the nearby interpretative centre, where guided tours begin *(tel: 046 25903)*.

Tara was once the seat of the high kings and the political and spiritual centre of Celtic Ireland. A passage tomb was built here some 4 000 years ago, and although the site continued to be important in early Christian times it was abandoned in 1022.

Trim

Tourist Information Office: Mill Street. Tel: 046 37111. Seasonal opening.

Situated on the River Boyne at a boundary of the Pale, this attractive town has some of the best medieval ruins in Ireland. **King John's Castle**, built by the Norman knight Hugh de Lacy in 1173, is the largest of its era in the country, covering 2 acres (0.8 hectares). Its formidable turreted keep, towers, long curtain wall and drawbridge made an impressive setting in the film *Braveheart*. Near by are the ruins of the medieval Royal Mint and a 13th-century Augustinian abbey. St Patrick's Cathedral, built in the 19th century, incorporates a 15th-century tower. On the outskirts of town are the magnificent **Butterstream Gardens** (*Kildalkey Road; tel: 046 36017; open: Apr–Sept; ££*), inspired by those at Sissinghurst in Kent. The visitor centre has an exhibition on medieval Trim.

Tullynally Castle

Castlepollard. Tel: 044 61159. Castle open: mid-June–mid-Aug 1430–1800; gardens open: May–Sept 1400–1800. ££.

The seat of the earls of Longford since 1655, Tullynally is Ireland's largest castle still in use as a family home. If you were to walk round the perimeter of this turreted and castellated pile you would cover nearly a quarter of a mile. The Gothic Revival additions to the original tower house were added in the 19th century. Interior highlights include the panelled dining room and collection of family portraits, the Victorian kitchens and laundries, and the extensive library. The grounds include a woodland walk, walled gardens, a grotto and two ornamental lakes.

The Pale

'The Pale' was a term that defined the territory under English control from the time of the Norman settlement until the early 17th century. The boundaries fluctuated, but its most extensive reach was from Dundalk in County Louth to Waterford City. Those within the Pale upheld English values, customs and interests. In Elizabethan times, Gaelic chieftains outside the area were allowed to keep their lands if they agreed to raise their heirs within the Pale. The expression 'beyond the Pale' still denotes those who operate on the fringe of society.

Eating and drinking

Birr

Spinners Bistro

Castle Street. Tel: 0509 21673. £–££.
Set in a 19th-century woollen store and decorated with red walls and paper lanterns, this bright, stylish bistro serves an international menu of light meals, creatively cooked and presented. Seafood, chicken, lamb, pasta and vegetarian dishes are cooked with fresh local ingredients, and there is a good selection of wines from around the world. It's a popular spot, so booking is advised.

Bray

Tree of Idleness

Sea Front. Tel: 286 3498. ££. Much-acclaimed Greek-Cypriot restaurant.

Dalkey

Mariner

Coliemore Road, just down the hill from the DART station. £. Friendly pub serving fresh fish, salmon, sea trout, burgers, chicken and other good pub meals.

PD's Woodhouse Barbecue Bistro

1 Coliemore Road. Tel: 01 284 9399. £–££. Fun restaurant serving excellent food, cooked on an open oak-burning grill.

Thai House

21 Railway Road. Tel: 01 284 7304. £££. Authentic Thai cuisine, cooked to perfection, has earned this restaurant a high reputation.

The Queen's

Castle Street. Tel: 01 285 4569. ££. An award-winning pub with a well-recommended restaurant.

Dun Laoghaire

Brasserie na Mara

1 Harbour Road. Tel: 280 6767. ££–£££. The restaurant, overlooking the harbour and adjacent to the DART station, is in what used to be a Victorian railway terminal. Renowned for fish delivered straight from the harbour to your plate, via the kitchen, it is highly popular – best to book.

Morel's Bistro

18 Glasthule Road. Tel: 230 0210. ££. Good wine, inspired cuisine and modest prices bring Dubliners back time and time again.

Krishna

Upstairs at 17 George's Street Lower. Tel: 280 1855. ££. Serves Northern Indian dishes. Evening opening is gratifyingly late – to 2330 Sun–Thur and 0030 Fri and Sat.

Drogheda

The Buttergate Restaurant

Millmount. Tel: 041 983 4759. ££. Booking advised. Set in the grounds of Millmount, this restaurant has an intimate atmosphere with spectacular views of Drogheda and the River Boyne. Seafood, steak, pork and vegetarian dishes are offered.

Sorrento's Ristorante

41 Shop Street. Tel: 041 984 5734. £. Cheerful Italian restaurant in the town centre serving a good selection of pizzas, pasta, steak and other dishes. Take-away also available.

Howth

The 16th-century **Abbey Tavern** (*££*), with flagstone floors and turf fire, which overlooks the harbour, serves delicious seafood – fish, crab, lobster and the famous Dublin Bay prawns. Also of high repute is the **King Sitric Fish Restaurant** on the East Pier (*£££*), where perfectly cooked fresh fish is served with organic vegetables. Inspired menus and a gift for unlikely pairings of foods – like dropping some whiskey into fish chowder – and getting it right makes **Adrian's** (*Abbey Street, ££*) an exciting place to eat.

Malahide

One of the features of **Smyth's of Malahide** (*12 New Street, lunch £, dinner ££*) is its American-style Fun Food Menu. Texas ribs and chargrilled steaks are specialities. **Charters** (*5 St James Terrace; open: evenings, closed Sun and Mon; £££*) offers classic French cuisine. For Italian tastes, try seafood or meat dishes at **Bon Appetit** (*9 St James Terrace; lunch ££, dinner £££*), or **Giovanni's** (*Townsend; lunch £, dinner ££*), which serves Italian and vegetarian food and steaks.

Shopping

Dun Laoghaire

For shopping and eating, you're spoilt for choice at the multi-storey shopping centre at the corner of Marine Road and Georges Street.

Nightlife

Craughwell's Bar and Lounge (*Castle Street, Birr*) is a friendly, family-run Irish pub with a cosy turf fire; on Saturday nights (and other times when the mood is right) the guitars come out and everyone sings along to traditional tunes.

Early Irish Art

Ireland's distance from continental Europe spared it from the ravages of the Dark Ages, and during those years this small island was in the vanguard of Christian culture. It was well suited to the development of rural monasteries, and thousands sought the rigid discipline of monastic life. Unlike their later European counterparts, the early Irish monasteries did not belong to large hierarchical orders but operated as isolated units. Many were tiny communities of two or three ascetics who prayed, studied and copied the gospels.

Others, such as Glendalough and Clonmacnoise, grew into large settlements as word of their holy founders spread. Learning, craftsmanship and the religious arts flourished, giving birth to what became the proud symbols of Irish culture: the great Celtic stone crosses; the beautiful decorated manuscripts; intricate chalices and reliquaries; and the unique round towers, which served as bell tower, storehouse and refuge in times of siege.

Irish high crosses

Although Celtic crosses are found elsewhere in the British Isles, the art of the decorative stone high cross reached its pinnacle in Ireland. Set in a base, its four arms encircled by a wheel, and capped by a shrine, it has become one of Ireland's most distinctive symbols. The majority were carved between the 8th and 12th centuries. The early crosses had ornamental carving, with the interlacing and spiralling patterns typical of other Celtic art. In the early 10th century figurative crosses with finely carved biblical scenes provided 'sermons in stone'. It is not known whether high crosses were once coloured, but traces of pigment on carved pieces from Europe, and the frequent use of colour in other Celtic art forms, suggests this is possible. Erected at cardinal points within the monasteries, they served as protective barriers against evil, as well as focal points for meeting and prayer. About 70 high crosses still stand around the country, many in their original positions. The finest are at Clonmacnoise, Monasterboice, Ahenny, Durrow and Kells.

Illuminating thoughts

The *Book of Kells*, exhibited in the Old Library at Trinity College (*see pages 51 and 70*) is acknowledged by many experts as the world's most beautiful illuminated manuscript. The *Book of Kells* is a copy of the four Gospels in Latin. Its pages measure 13in by 9in, and some contain no more than a single initial letter. Beautifully calligraphed, the pages were illuminated with exquisite designs and colourful scenes, often painted with real gold. The books were bound in leather, embellished with gold, silver and precious stones.

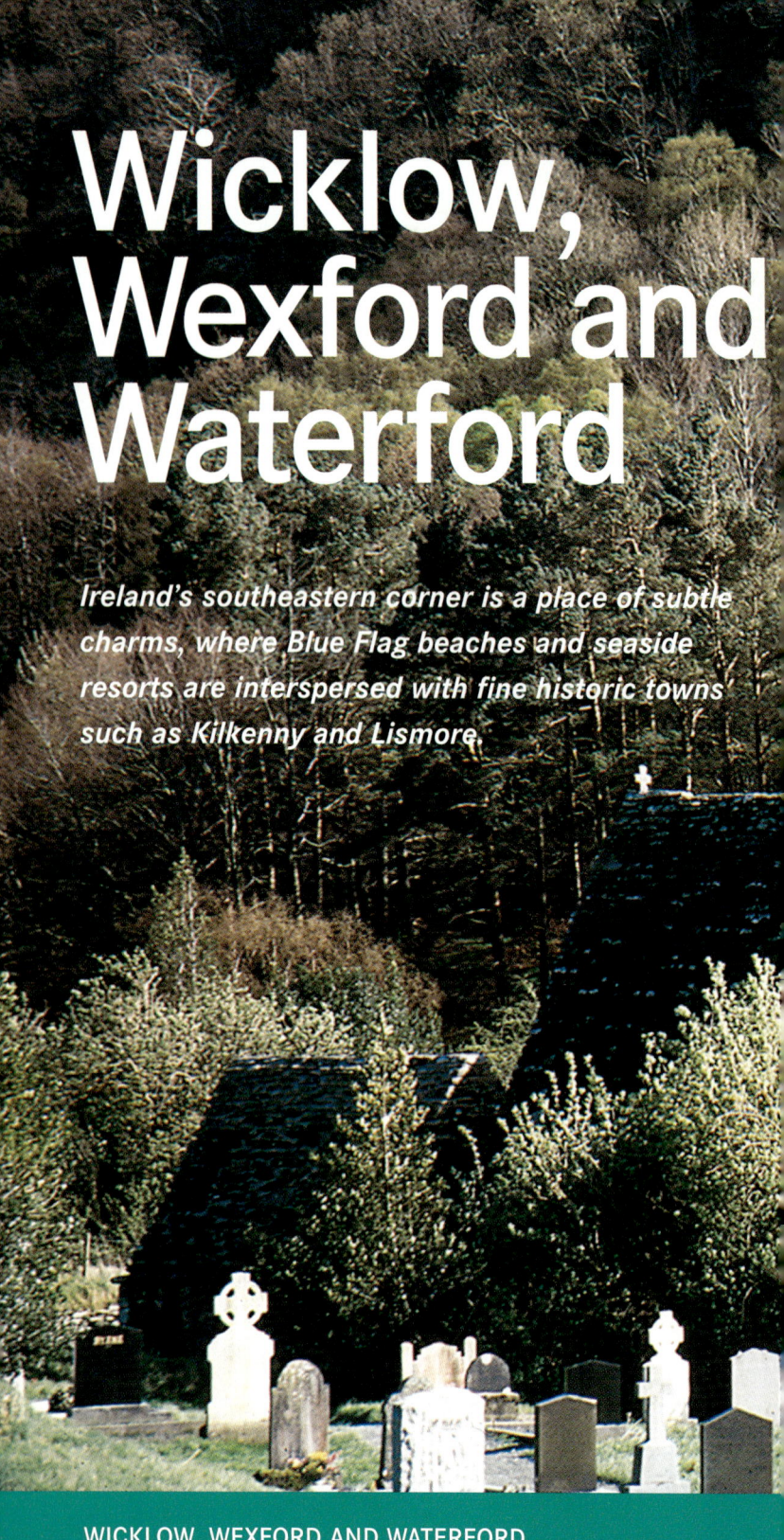

Wicklow, Wexford and Waterford

Ireland's southeastern corner is a place of subtle charms, where Blue Flag beaches and seaside resorts are interspersed with fine historic towns such as Kilkenny and Lismore.

WICKLOW, WEXFORD AND WATERFORD

BEST OF

Wicklow, Wexford and Waterford

Getting there: the southeastern corner of Ireland is well served by train services from Dublin. The main line runs down the east coast via Wicklow and Wexford to the port town of Rosslare, and from Rosslare west to Waterford, Carrick-on-Suir and Cahir. Even so, you will need a car for maximum flexibility.

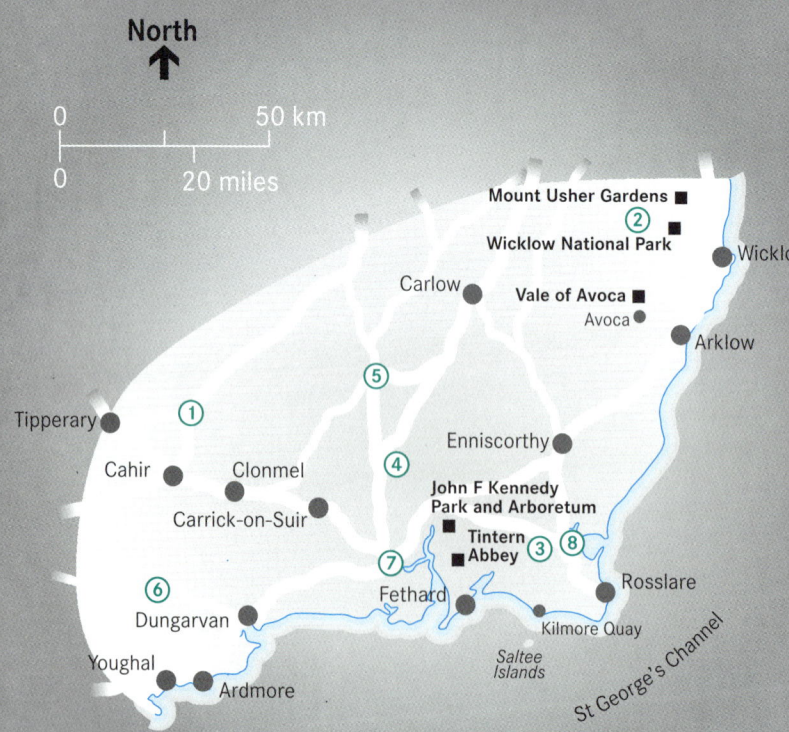

North

0   50 km

0   20 miles

Mount Usher Gardens ■
②
Wicklow National Park ■   ● Wicklo

Carlow   Vale of Avoca ■
     Avoca ●
       ● Arklow

⑤

Tipperary ●   ①

Cahir ●   Clonmel ●   Enniscorthy ●
    ④
Carrick-on-Suir ●   John F Kennedy
      Park and Arboretum ■
      Tintern Abbey ■
     ⑦   ③ ⑧

⑥   Fethard ●   ● Rosslare
Dungarvan ●   Kilmore Quay ●

Youghal ●   Saltee Islands
    ● Ardmore   St George's Channel

① *Cashel*

Visit the atmospheric ruins of Cashel cathedral, sitting on top of its rocky stronghold. Seat of the early Irish kings of Munster and home to a flourishing monastic community, this medieval complex has some of Ireland's best-preserved Romanesque architecture. **Pages 92–3**

② *Glendalough*

Dotted around the beautiful wooded 'Valley of the Two Lakes' is a group of early Irish ruins dating from St Kevin's 6th-century monastic foundation, including round towers, high crosses and hermits' cells. **Page 95**

③ *Irish National Heritage Park*

Come here to learn about life in the past, from the earliest prehistoric passage graves to Celtic farms, complete with animals, and reconstructions of the longships used by Ireland's Viking settlers. **Page 96**

④ *Jerpoint Abbey*

One of Ireland's finest monastic ruins, Jerpoint Abbey is covered in sculptures that bring the medieval period to life – knights, dragons and courtly ladies are interspersed with devils, monsters and saints. **Page 97**

⑤ *Kilkenny*

Georgian buildings with colourfully painted façades line the streets of one of Ireland's most attractive cities, renowned for its castle, for Smithwick's beer and for its annual arts festival. **Pages 98–9**

⑥ *Lismore*

Pre-Raphaelite stained-glass windows in St Carthach's Cathedral tell the story of the founding of this pretty town on the River Blackwater, with riverside walks and sumptuous castle gardens. **Pages 100–1**

⑦ *Waterford*

Known internationally for its Waterford Crystal Factory, Waterford is a town of elegant Georgian houses encircled by well-preserved medieval walls, with a Viking heritage that is well illustrated in the local museum. **Pages 104–5**

⑧ *Wexford*

Traditional Irish music and grand opera combine at Wexford's famous festival, held in a handsome town that sits on an estuary renowned for overwintering birds. **Pages 106–7**

Ardmore

The resort village of Ardmore, with its magnificent golden **beach**, is also one of the oldest religious sites in Europe. St Declan brought Christianity to this region in 416, well before the arrival of his famous successor, St Patrick. The ruins of the **monastery** he founded are set on the hillside, overlooking the beach. Most of the buildings date from the 12th century.

Healing properties

Near the shore at Ardmore stands a large glacial boulder. Local legend claims it was borne across the sea from Rome in the wake of St Declan's ship, carrying a bell that the holy man had forgotten. It also has healing powers, and those who manage to crawl underneath it are said to be cured of the pains of rheumatism.

The Romanesque cathedral has some outstanding carvings of biblical scenes on the exterior of the west wall. They depict the Adoration of the Magi, the Judgement of King Solomon, and the Archangel Michael weighing the souls of the dead. In the chancel are two notched ogham stones. The **round tower** beside the cathedral is one of Ireland's finest specimens, tapering up to a height of 95ft (29m). There is a spectacular cliff walk beyond the village.

Arklow

Tourist Information Office: tel: 0402 32484; fax: 0402 39773.

The Vikings founded a settlement here at the mouth of the River Avoca in the 9th century, and today Arklow is a popular resort with beaches, boating and a golf course. The town sprawls along its long, narrow main street, dominated by the spire of St Saviour's Church. Arklow's seafaring history is recalled in the **Maritime Museum** (*St Mary's Road; tel: 0402 32868; open: May–Sept, Mon–Sat 1000–1300, 1400–1700; Oct–Apr, Mon–Fri only; ££*). Down by the harbour, the **Arklow Pottery Factory** (*tel: 0402 39442; open: weekdays 0900–1700, weekends 1000–1700*) is Ireland's largest, and gives guided tours.

Vale of Avoca

This delightful vale, where the Rivers Avonmore and Avonbeg meet, inspired the Irish Romantic poet Thomas Moore (1779–1852) to pen *The Meeting of the Waters* in 1807. Today the spot is marked by a pub, called The Meeting, renowned for its traditional music sessions. **Avoca** village, 2 miles (3km) beyond, is the location for the BBC television series *Ballykissangel*; thus the Church of SS Mary and Patrick, built in 1862, and the local pub may look familiar to some visitors. **Avoca Handweavers** (*tel: 0402 35105; shop open: daily 0930–1730; mill open: weekdays 0800–1630*) occupies the oldest working mill in Ireland, dating from 1723. You can take a guided tour and watch the weavers creating their beautiful woven tweeds.

Avondale House and Forest Park

Tel: 0404 46111. Open: daily June–Sept 1000–1800, Oct–May 1100–1700. Parking ££.

Charles Stewart Parnell, a hero for his part in the struggle for Irish independence, was born here in 1846. Parnell was a Protestant landowner, and he fought passionately for tenants' land rights and Home Rule for Ireland from his parliamentary seat at Westminster. He won several reforms, but was blocked by northern Protestants, who feared Catholic domination, in his efforts to achieve Home Rule. His shining political career was brought down by the scandal surrounding his affair with a married woman, Mrs Kitty O'Shea. The house, restored to its mid-19th-century décor, is a museum filled with memorabilia of his career and personal life, including some of his love letters to Kitty. It is set in 500 acres (200 hectares) of parkland along the River Avonmore, with miles of woodland paths to explore.

Cahir

Tourist Information Office: tel: 052 41453. Open: May–Sept.

The town of Cahir dates mainly from the 18th century; some of its best architecture can be seen in the Mall opposite the castle and in the town square, including **St Paul's Church** (1817) to the east of the square, designed by John Nash. **Cahir Castle**, standing on its own island in the River Suir, dominates this attractive town (*tel: 052 41011; open: mid-Mar–mid-June and mid Sept–mid Oct, daily 0930–1730; mid-June–mid Sept, daily 0900–1930; mid-Oct–mid-Mar, daily 0930–1630; ££*). It was built by the powerful Butler family in the 15th century, on the site of an earlier Norman fortress. The highlights of the castle, which was known as the 'bulwark of Munster' in the 16th century, are its defensive features, including the curtain wall, the working portcullis and the holes for pouring boiling oil upon the enemy. In 1650, however, the threat of Cromwell's cannon proved too great and the garrison surrendered, leaving this splendid fortress intact. The Great Hall and other rooms are restored, with period furnishings.

On the outskirts of town – and easily reached by a half-hour walk along the river – is the delightful **Swiss Cottage** (*tel: 052 41144; open: Mar–Apr and Oct–Nov, Tue–Sun 1000–1300, 1400–1630 or 1700; May–Sept, daily 1000–1800; ££*), designed by John Nash in the early 19th century as an idyllic thatch-roofed retreat for Lord Cahir.

Carrick-on-Suir

This old market town enjoys a fine setting alongside a beautiful stretch of the River Suir. Its medieval bridge and winding streets survive, though little remains of the 13th-century friary. The Tholsel on Main Street now houses a heritage centre. The town's highlight is **Ormonde Castle** (*tel: 051 640787; open: mid-June–Sept, daily 0930–1830; ££*), an Elizabethan mansion and the only one of its kind in Ireland. 'Black Tom' Butler, 10th Earl of Ormonde, built the graceful gabled manor house in 1565, adjoining the battlemented 15th-century keep of his ancestors. He was a supporter and cousin to Queen Elizabeth I and built the house in hopes of a royal visit, which never materialised. The interior is outstanding for its stucco decorations, particularly the Long Gallery with its heraldic ceiling crests and medallions, and elaborately carved fireplaces.

Cashel

Tourist Information Office: Town Hall, Main Street; tel: 062 61333. Open: Apr–Sept, Mon–Sat 0900–1800; Sun in July–Aug.

Rising 200ft (61m) above the plain and topped by a cluster of historic ruins, the **Rock of Cashel** is truly an impressive sight *(tel: 062 61437; open: mid-Mar–mid-June 0930–1730; mid-June–mid-Sept daily 0900–1930; mid-Sept–mid-Mar 0930–1630; ££)*. The kings of Munster ruled their lands from atop this limestone outcrop from around 370 until 1101, when it was granted to the Church. The Bishop's Walk makes an atmospheric approach to the Rock; it takes about 10 minutes from the town below. The entrance to the ecclesiastical site is through the **Vicar's Choral Hall**, where there is a museum containing St Patrick's Cross; the base in which it is set is reputed to be the coronation stone of the Munster kings. **Cormac's Chapel**, consecrated in 1134, is a masterpiece of medieval architecture, with its steep stone roof and decorated 11th-century stone sarcophagus. A gilt copper crozier found inside is now in the National Museum in Dublin. The first cathedral, founded in 1169, was burned in 1495 by the Earl of Kildare. He was hauled to justice before Henry VII, who pardoned him when he explained that he 'thought the archbishop was in it'. The new cathedral suffered the same fate at the hands of Cromwell's troops, after which it was deconsecrated in 1647. Among its highlights are the north transept, with a series of sculptures depicting the Apostles and saints; the octagonal staircase turret beside the central tower, which leads to defensive passages in the walls; the round tower; and the views from atop the central tower.

The **Brian Boru Heritage Centre** (*tel: 062 61122; open: Mon–Fri 0900–1700; Folk Theatre performances June–Sept at 2100; £*) at the base of the rock is named after Brian Boru, Ireland's first high king, who was crowned here in 977. It has exhibits on Irish culture and traditional entertainment in the evenings. In Cashel town, the **Cashel of the Kings Heritage Centre** (*Town Hall; tel: 062 62511; open: June–Aug, daily 0930–1900; rest of the year, daily 0930–1700; guided*

tours of the town can be arranged) is adjacent to the tourist office and has a scale model of the town as it was in the 1600s. The **Bolton Library** (*tel: 062 61232; open: June–Aug, Mon–Fri 1100–1630; other times by appointment; ££*), in the grounds of St John the Baptist Cathedral, has several exhibits from its extensive collection of rare books and manuscripts on display.

Cashel Folk Village (*Dominic Street; tel: 062 62525; open: Mar–Apr, daily 1000–1800; May–Feb, daily 0930–1630*) has replicas of 18th to early 20th-century buildings and a range of memorabilia.

Clonmel

Tourist Information Office: town centre; tel: 052 22960. Open: all year.

Clonmel, the county seat of Tipperary and one of Ireland's largest inland towns, occupies a pretty position beneath the Comeragh Mountains on the River Suir. Old mills form a pleasing façade along the quays and near by is the **Franciscan Friary**, with interesting monuments inside. The Court House, designed by Sir Richard Morrison, and St Mary's Protestant Church, partly enclosed by the old town walls, are also noteworthy. Clonmel is also a famous centre for greyhound races. The towpath that runs along the river for 12 miles (19km) between Clonmel and Carrick-on-Suir makes for a scenic day's walk.

Fethard

This tiny Tipperary town is still partly enclosed by sections of its **14th-century town walls**. Holy Trinity Church (13th century) has many interesting tombs and monuments and its west tower is one of three medieval fortress towers that still stand in the town centre. The town hall in Market Square is housed in a merchant's house dating to 1640. A well-preserved Augustinian friary, dating from the 14th century and re-opened in 1823, lies at one end of town. The Presentation Convent was designed by Pugin and Ashlin in 1862.

St Kevin

Many stories are told about the asceticism of St Kevin. He is said to have stood in the cold waters of the Upper Lake with outstretched arms until birds built nests in his hands. Women who tried to seduce him in his rocky cell were beaten with nettles or thrown into the lake.

Glendalough

Tourist Information Office: tel: 0404 45588.

Glendalough, one of Ireland's most important monastic sites, was founded by St Kevin, a descendant of one of Leinster's ruling families, in the 6th century. His reputation as a holy man grew and he attracted many followers. He became abbot of the monastery in 570, and the settlement flourished for more than six centuries after his death in 618, despite repeated raids and rebuilding. English forces reduced it to ruins in 1398, but Glendalough remained a great pilgrimage site well into the 19th century. The ruins of Glendalough are spread along 2 miles (3km) of a peaceful wooded valley that is part of the Wicklow National Park. The cathedral, St Kevin's Church and several smaller churches are approached through the granite-arched gateway behind the visitor centre. Here, too, is the famous round tower, built of mica-slate and granite and rising some 98ft (30m). The visitor centre (*tel: 0404 45325; open: daily 0930–1800 summer; 0930–1700 winter; £*) has exhibits and a good audio-visual programme. St Kevin's Cell, Reefert Church and other sites are set around the Upper Lake. They are accessible from a separate car park or on foot from the visitor centre, making a lovely walk on a fine day.

Irish National Heritage Park

3 miles (5km) from Wexford town at Ferrycarrig, at the junction of the N11 and N25. Tel: 053 20733. Open: Mar–Oct, daily 0930–1830. £££.

The Irish National Heritage Park presents 9 000 years of Irish history through a series of reconstructed dwellings that illustrate life from mesolithic to Norman times. A pleasant walk through the woodlands leads you to a camp site dating from 7000 BC, an early Irish farmstead (children will enjoy the animals here), a portal tomb, a ring fort, monastic settlement and horizontal mill. The *crannog* – a homestead built on an artificial island – is very atmospheric, surrounded by its reed-filled lake. There is also a Viking boathouse, a round tower and a Norman motte and bailey. The park is extremely well done, with realistic exhibits that are informative without being overwhelming, and can be easily covered in a few hours.

John F Kennedy Park and Arboretum

7 1/2 miles (12km) south of New Ross. Tel: 051 388171. Open: daily. ££.

Set on a hill to the south of New Ross, the John F Kennedy Park and Arboretum commemorates one of Ireland's most famous descendants, the former president of the United States who was assassinated in 1963. The 623-acre (252-hectare) site contains more than 4 500 species of trees and shrubs from around the world. There are wonderful panoramic views from the hillsides, walking paths and nature trails, picnic areas, a visitor centre and, in summer, pony and trap rides. The Kennedy Homestead at nearby Dunganstown, where JFK's great-grandfather lived before emigrating in the 19th century, has been restored and is now open to visitors. It contains a collection of JFK memorabilia.

Jerpoint Abbey

One mile (1.5km) south of Thomastown. Tel: 056 24623. Open: Mar–May and mid-Sept–Nov, Wed–Mon 1000–1700 or 1600; June–mid-Sept, daily 0930–1830. ££.

Jerpoint Abbey is one of Ireland's finest monastic ruins. It was founded in 1158, but most of the existing structures date from 1180, when the Cistercians from Baltinglass colonised the site. The church contains many fine 13th to 16th-century tombs featuring effigies of abbots and knights. In the cloister arcade, each pier is finely carved with figures ranging from saints to grotesques. The visitor centre has exhibits on the region's high crosses and the abbey's medieval tiles.

Johnstown Castle

3 miles (5km) south of Wexford Town. Tel: 053 42888. Open: daily 1000–1700. ££.

The ancestral seat of the Esmondes, Johnstown Castle dates back to Norman times. It now houses a college and research centre, but the delightful gardens, lakes and picnic areas are accessible. The Irish Agricultural Museum is housed in the castle outbuildings. It contains displays of Irish country furniture, along with regional farming exhibits.

Kilkenny

Kilkenny is one of Ireland's finest cities, full of medieval treasures and lined with brightly painted Victorian-style pubs (Smithwick's beer has been brewed in Kilkenny since 1710, when the Smithwick family took over the medieval St Francis Abbey and converted it into a brewery). The town is made for walking, with many picturesque streets such as High Street, with its 18th-century Tholsel and clock tower. The medieval alleyways, called 'slips', running off it are also fun to explore, such as the Butter Slip, once lined with market stalls selling butter. There is a wealth of architecture, from Georgian façades to Tudor features, much of it sporting the local black limestone called Kilkenny marble.

St Canice founded a monastic school here in the 6th century, from which Kilkenny (*Kil Cainneach* or 'Church of Canice') takes its name. **St Canice's Cathedral** (*open: Easter–Oct, Mon–Sat 0900–1300, 1400–1800, Sun 1400–1800; rest of the year 'til 1600. £*), built in the 13th century, is the second-longest cathedral in Ireland. It, too, has a splendid hammer beam roof with carved wood figures, ornate carved choir stalls and beautiful lancet windows. It is studded with magnificent and intricately sculpted stone tombs, under which many bishops and members of the powerful Anglo-Norman family, the Butlers, are laid to rest. Other treasures include the finely carved west door, the 12th-century baptismal font and the ancient stone throne, St Kieran's Chair. You can climb the round tower for a fine view over the town.

The Butlers came to power here in the 12th century and built the formidable **Kilkenny Castle** (*tel: 056 21450; open: Apr–May, daily 1030–1700; June–Sept, daily 1000–1900; Oct–Mar, reduced hours and closed Mon; admission by guided tour only; last tour one hour before closing; ££*), set in parkland and commanding a fine position along the

River Nore. Built in the 1190s, its Norman features have been enhanced by later Gothic Revival-style alterations. Its highlight is the Long Gallery, stretching 150ft (46m) with a magnificent oak hammer beam ceiling and skylights. The Butler gallery, with its ornate painted ceiling, houses a modern art collection.

The **Black Abbey**, another of Kilkenny's five medieval abbeys, was founded by the black-robed Dominicans in 1225. The church has stunning stained glass, some as old as the 14th century. More sombre features are the 13th-century stone coffins of victims of the Black Death.

Getting there: Tourist Information Office: located in the Shee Alms House, Rose Inn Street; tel: 056 51500; fax: 056 63955. Open: Mon–Sat 0900–1700; 'til 1800 Apr, May and Sept; 'til 2000 July–Aug; also open Sun 1100–1700 May–Sept.

Kilmore Quay

This picturesque village is one of the main fishing ports in the southeast. It is known for its old-world thatched cottages, unique to the area with their thick whitewashed walls and hip and gable ends. At the harbour, the lightship *Guillemot* has been turned into a **maritime museum** (*tel: 053 29655; open: daily, June–Sept; ££*). The new marina is a popular angling and boating centre. **Ballyteigue Burrow** is an outstanding system of sand dunes that stretches for $5^{1}/_{2}$ miles (9km) along the coast from Kilmore Quay to Cullenstown; the western end is a national nature reserve that protects thousands of wild flowers and butterflies.

Offshore are the **Saltee Islands**, two large granite outcrops that form one of Ireland's primary bird sanctuaries. They are particularly significant for their colonies of breeding cormorants. Boat trips from Kilmore Quay operate in good weather, or ask the local fishermen at the harbour.

Lismore

This delightful small town on the River Blackwater has more to repay a visit than first meets the eye. Lismore's

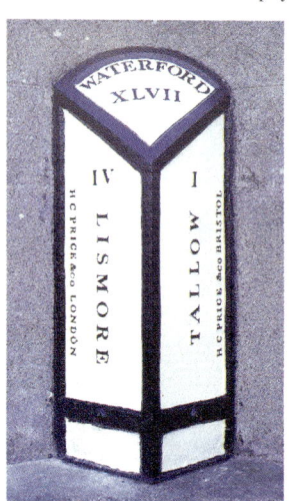

luminous history is told in the **Heritage Centre** in the Courthouse (*tel: 058 54975; open: Apr, May, Sept and Oct, Mon–Sat 0930–1800, Sun 1000–1730; June–Aug, Mon–Sat 0930–1800, Sun 1000–1730; Nov–Mar, Mon–Fri 0930–1730; ££*). From the 7th to 12th centuries it was a centre of religion and learning, renowned throughout Europe. Two treasures – the Lismore Crozier, now in the National Museum in Dublin, and *The Book of Lismore*, a 15th-century manuscript – were discovered hidden in the castle in 1814.

The **castle**, erected by King John in 1185, was rebuilt in the 19th century by the 6th Duke of Devonshire, and it remains the family's Irish home. Its grey stone bulk towers over the village from its lofty perch. Only the gardens are open to the public, but these lush grounds are well worth a visit, especially in late spring when the magnolias and camellias are blooming (*tel: 058 54424; open: May–Sept, daily 1345–1645; ££*). Not to be missed is **St Carthach's Cathedral**, approached along a path lined with aged trees. It was built in the 17th century, incorporating parts of an earlier church. Two stained-glass windows in the south transept are by the Pre-Raphaelite artist, Sir Edward Burne-Jones.

Within these walls

In Ireland, town walls often served to keep foreign invaders in, not out. Medieval cities in County Cork were 'closed boroughs' and had separate 'Irish towns' outside the walls. The native Irish had to obtain special permission to enter the city gates or trade within. In 1366 the Crown enacted the hated Statutes of Kilkenny. Under these laws, intermarriage was high treason and English settlers could lose their lands for speaking Irish, wearing Irish dress, or giving their children Irish names.

Mount Usher Gardens

Ashford. Tel: 0404 40205. Open: Mar–Nov, daily 1030–1800. ££.

These beautiful gardens, spreading over 20 acres (8 hectares) alongside the River Varty, were originally laid out by Edward Walpole, a Dublin businessman, in 1868. The natural terrain enhances their wild, romantic style, and suspension bridges span the winding waterway with its mesmerising cascades. Over the years, the Walpole family introduced many exotic species from around the world, which flourished in the sheltered environment. Today there are about 5 000 species, including eucalyptus, magnolias, camellias and giant rhododendrons.

Rosslare

Tourist Information Office: Rosslare Ferry Terminal. Tel: 053 33622; fax: 053 33421. The office is open year-round to service all sailings. Rosslare-Kilrane Tourist Information Office: Kilrane. Tel: 053 33232. Open: May–mid-Sept.

George Bernard Shaw was 'lost in dreams' in this picturesque village, which lies 5 miles (8km) north of its more famous harbour. Its beautiful beach – 6 miles (10km) long and golden, with an EU Blue Flag – and the fact that it's one of the sunniest places in the country, makes it a popular resort. It also has a championship golf course. Rosslare Harbour became the area's principal port when Wexford's harbour silted up and could no longer handle the big ships. Today it is a busy terminal, serving car and passenger ferries.

Tintern Abbey

Tel: 051 397124. Forest walks and guided tours: daily, July–Aug.

Around the year 1200, William Marshal, Earl of Pembroke, and his wife were sailing to Wexford from Britain when they were caught in a ferocious storm. He vowed that if he survived the journey he would build an abbey on the spot where he landed in safety. The ship skirted treacherous rocks before beaching itself at this pretty creek, where the earl built the abbey in thanksgiving. It was named after Tintern Abbey in Wales, which sent Cistercian monks to occupy it. It passed into residential use after the Dissolution of the monasteries in 1536. Restoration is in progress, but the ruins are accessible.

Waterford

Set alongside the River Suir (pronounced 'Sure'), Waterford is a busy, vibrant city with traces of its great heritage woven around its waterfront and modern central shopping district. The attractive quays with their central Victorian clock tower run for nearly a mile along the river.

Artefacts from the city's Viking origins and medieval times are displayed at the **Waterford Heritage Museum** (*Greyfriar's Street; tel: 051 871227; open: Apr–Oct, daily 1000–1700; Nov–Mar, weekdays only; ££*). At the east end of the quays is the bulky **Reginald's Tower** (*tel: 051 873501; open: June–Aug, daily 1000–2000; May and Sept, weekdays 1000–1700, weekends 1400–1700; ££*), with walls 10ft (3m) thick; it was used as a residence by Anglo-Norman kings. Their leader Strongbow had captured the city in 1170, married the daughter of the Leinster king, and succeeded to the throne.

Some of the city's finest Georgian architecture can be seen along The Mall, including town houses, the City Hall and the adjacent Bishop's Palace. The neo-classical **Christ Church Cathedral**, with its Corinthian colonnade, was built in

Take to the river

On a fine day, a cruise along the River Suir is a good way to enjoy Waterford's skyline. Galley Cruises (tel: 051 421723) leaves daily at 1500 during June–Aug from the quay (weather permitting).

the 1770s by the local architect John Roberts. Inside, a gruesome effigy of a rotting corpse marks the tomb of James Rice. Roberts also designed **Holy Trinity**, the city's Catholic cathedral, with a more subdued façade but highly ornate interior. It's worth seeking out the remnants of Waterford's **city walls**, some of the best preserved in Ireland. The finest section can be found near the watch-tower on Castle Street.

The first Waterford glasshouse began producing its exquisite patterned glassware in 1783. On the outskirts of town, the **Waterford Crystal Factory and Visitor Centre** (*1 mile (2km) outside Waterford on the N25 to Cork; tel: 051 373311; tours Apr–Oct, daily 0830–1600; Nov–Mar, weekdays 0900–1515; showrooms open: Jan–Feb, weekdays 0900–1700; Mar–Oct, daily 0830–1800; Nov–Mar, daily 0900–1700; ££*), now the largest of its kind in the world, is a popular attraction. Guided tours take visitors through the production area to watch the craftsmen at work.

Getting there: Tourist Information Office: The Quay. Tel: 051 875788, fax: 051 877388. Open: Apr–Sept, Mon–Sat 0900–1800; Sun 1100–1700 in Jul–Aug; weekdays only in winter 0900–1700.

105

Wexford Town

This historic county town was founded by the Vikings, who named it Waesfjord, the 'harbour of the mud flats'. It flourished as a major port until the harbour silted over in the 19th century. Wexford is one of the more atmospheric of Ireland's larger heritage towns, with its Viking street plan, and medieval alleys such as Keyser and Oyster lanes, running between Main Street and the quays.

The **Westgate Heritage Centre** (*tel: 053 46506*), housed in the only surviving gateway of the old Norman town walls, traces the town's history. The centre also organises **walking tours** of Wexford Town, which take place in July and Aug (*Mon–Sat 1100 and 1430*); there are also *ad hoc* tours leaving each evening from the Talbot Hotel (*tel: 053 41081*).

Opposite the tourist information office in the Crescent is a bronze statue of **Commodore John Barry**, a Wexford native who became a naval hero and father of the American Navy. Augustus Welby Pugin, the 19th-century English architect who built Nottingham Cathedral and the Roman Catholic church of St Giles in Cheadle, Staffordshire, spent many

holidays in Wexford and designed a large number of churches in the county, including **St Peter's College Chapel** in Wexford Town (others include St Aidan's Cathedral in Enniscorthy and churches at Gorey, Ramsgrange, Bree and Tagoat). The square known as the **Bull Ring** recalls the bull-baiting that occurred here in Norman times. On Main Street the **Cornmarket**, a striking 18th-century market house, is now the Wexford Arts Centre. Near by are the ruins of **Selskar Abbey**, a 12th-century Augustinian priory where Henry II is said to have done penance for ordering the murder of Thomas à Becket. The mudflats to the east of town contain the 250-acre (100-hectare) **Wexford Wildfowl Reserve** (*open: mid-Apr–Sept, daily 0900–1800; Oct–mid-Apr, daily 1000–1700; £*), wintering ground for thousands of geese and other species of birds.

Getting there: Tourist Information Office: Crescent Quay. Tel: 053 23111; fax: 053 41743. Open year-round.

By Hook or by Crooke

As the Anglo-Normans battled for a foothold in the southeast of Ireland in 1170, their leader, Strongbow, vowed he would take Waterford 'by Hook or by Crooke'. He was referring to two heavily fortified defences at Waterford Harbour: the Tower of Hook on the Wexford side and Crooke Castle, across the water near Passage East. He succeeded, and unlike the ruined towers, his words are still in use today.

WICKLOW, WEXFORD AND WATERFORD

Wicklow National Park

Education Centre, Bolger's Cottage, Upper Lake, Glendalough. Tel: 0404 45425 (summer); 0404 45338 (winter). Open: May–Aug, daily 1000–1800; Apr and Sept, weekends only.

Travellers heading south from Dublin will experience an abrupt change of scenery as they pass from pretty pastureland, gently wooded slopes and river valleys to the sweeping expanse of desolate moorland at the centre of the Wicklow range. The only sign of civilisation is the signposts at the four-way crossroads known as **Sally Gap**, which is surrounded by a vast blanket bog. This is part of the Wicklow National Park, which covers some 49 421 acres (20 000 hectares), encompassing forests, boglands, lakes and nature reserves. The Education Centre has information on the park and offers summer lecture programmes and activities.

From Sally Gap the old military road goes to Laragh and Glendalough, 13 miles (21km) away. After a few miles of rough tarmac, you pass through a stretch of forest that opens up to a magnificent view of the **Glenmacnass Waterfall** tumbling into the broad valley below. The road descends to Laragh (pronounced 'Laura'), a favourite spot for the many ramblers and cyclists who pass through the area; in summer, tables are set out on the village green and some of the little cottages operate makeshift tea rooms.

The potato

Sir Walter Raleigh is said to have planted Ireland's first potato, brought back from the New World, at his home in Youghal, County Cork, in the 1580s. In celebration, the town holds an annual potato festival.

Youghal

Visitor Centre: Market Square. Tel: 024 92390 or 92447. Heritage Centre (££) open daily; guided walking tours daily in season at 1100 and 1500; out of season by arrangement.

This charming heritage town grew up at the wide mouth of the River Blackwater. Its name, pronounced 'Yawl', comes from the yew woodlands that once covered the area. Occupied from Viking times, under the English it became a 'closed borough' – with the Irish population living outside the town walls. Youghal's **Market Square** may look vaguely familiar to film buffs. It was one of the locations used by the director John Huston for his production of *Moby Dick*. The film crew's watering hole was Moby Dick's Pub, where you can still enjoy a brew. Gregory Peck, never out of character in this role as Captain Ahab, signed the guestbook 'Death to Moby Dick'.

The Clock Gate straddles the main street of the brightly painted old town. The Watergate connects the town to the picturesque quayside. Among the sights of interest are Myrtle Grove, a Tudor manor house once lived in by Sir Walter Raleigh; St Mary's Collegiate Church which dates from the 11th century; the Dutch-style Red House; medieval Alms Houses; priory ruins; and remnants of the old town walls. With its long, sandy Blue Flag beach and fun fair, Youghal is a popular seaside resort.

Eating and drinking

Cashel

Even if you don't stay there, drop into the **Cashel Palace Hotel** (*Main Street; tel: 062 62707, fax: 062 61521*) for tea to see its fine interior carving and panelling. The Queen Anne-style building was designed in 1730 by Edward Lovett Pearce, who also built Dublin's Houses of Parliament, and was a former archbishops' residence. For something very special, head for **Chez Hans** (*beside the Rock of Cashel; tel: 062 61177; closed Sun and Mon*), where local food is treated with the respect it deserves: people come a long way to eat the risotto of Dublin Bay prawns and the herb-crusted lamb.

Cashel Blue

To any cheese lover, Cashel means the gorgeous creamy blue cheese produced in Fethard by Lane and Louis Grubb. Cashel Blue is sold throughout Ireland, but nowhere else does it taste quite so right as in the region where it is made: look for the distinctive gold wrapping in local grocers' shops.

Kilkenny

The Hibernian

33 Patrick Street. Tel: 056 71888. ££. You will feel like a millionaire in this richly renovated bank building, right in the heart of town, a stone's throw from Kilkenny Castle. The splendid interior retains its stained-glass windows and grand central staircase. The panelled Victorian banking hall is now a spacious breakfast, lunch and tea room. There are bars, a restaurant and on-site parking.

Pordylo's Restaurant and Wine Bar

Butterslip Lane. Tel: 056 70660. £–££. This atmospheric restaurant, located down a medieval lane off the High Street, serves pasta, steaks and seafood fresh from Dunmore East. The chef's world travels are reflected in the menu, which features a curry dish, a Mexican dish, monkfish and chicken blackened in Cajun spices, and the fabulous Moroccan seafood pot, served on lemon couscous. The restaurant is set above the well-stocked ground-floor wine bar, in a building dating from 1602, which sports its original oak beam ceiling and stone walls. The lighting is low, the service attentive and the food delicious.

Nightlife

The **Wexford Opera Festival**, held annually in late October/early November, attracts international artists and opera buffs. This prestigious event stages three lesser-known operas, along with exhibitions and fringe events, over 18 days at the Theatre Royal. *Tel: 053 22144 (booking office) or 053 22400 (administration).*

Rosslare

Kelly's Resort Hotel.
Tel: 053 32114. Closed Dec to Feb. ££.
If the name conjures up visions of soggy
overcooked boarding house food, you
are in for a surprise. Making the most
of all the fresh fish to be had in this
port town, the chef here serves up a
varied menu of fish dishes from around
the world – from Spanish-style cod to
Chinese squid. Good steaks and delicious
puddings are taken for granted.

Waterford

The Wine Vault
*High Street. Tel: 051 853444. Closed
Sun. ££.* As you would expect from a
bistro of this name, the wine list here
is exceptional, both in terms of value
and in variety. The good and simple
food is well chosen to complement the
wines, and there is nothing snobby
about the place – the perfect wine bar
in which to relax and digest the events
of the day.

Wexford

Ferrycarrig Hotel
*Ferrycarrig Bridge. Tel: 053 20999.
££–£££.* Set just outside the bustle of
Wexford Town, the sweeping views of
the River Slaney estuary bring instant
tranquillity. The bright, casual bistro
with its coloured sailcloth canopies is
set alongside the water. The food is
excellent – crisp chilled salad bar, an
imaginative set menu and a good
variety of à la carte dishes – and
reasonably priced. There is also the
romantic Tides Restaurant for more
intimate dining, the lively Dry Dock
Bar, and a residents' lounge that will
make you think you've died and gone
to the Caribbean.

Shopping

Avoca

Tourists used to go to Avoca to see **Avoca Handweavers** and to buy their lovely
tweed suits, coats and jackets. They still do, but another reason is that the small
village in wooded, hilly countryside is now famous as the setting of the TV soap
Ballykissangel. As well as gorgeous clothes and accessories, Avoca Handweavers
sells crafts and gifts and has a restaurant. If you can't see what you want here, call
at the company's outlet at Kilmacanogue, near Bray, on the way back to Dublin.

Kilkenny

Kilkenny is a centre for crafts and design, and a great range of original works is
produced here, from glass, pottery and precious metals to leather and textiles. The
Kilkenny Design Centre, renowned throughout Ireland, carries a good range. It
is located opposite the castle on The Parade (*tel: 056 22118; open: daily 0900–1800;
Jan–Mar, closed Sun*). The **National Crafts Council** (*tel: 056 21037*), located in
the building, or the tourist office can help you seek out individual workshops.

Art and architecture

Ireland's rich architectural history begins in ancient times, with the megalithic portal tombs (or dolmens), passage tombs and court cairns erected between 3000 and 2000 BC. Their name derives from the passage that leads from the entrance to the inner burial chamber. Although they are called 'tombs', these massive structures had other purposes than mere burial, and were likely to have served as a focal point for a tribe or group. The large number of stones that have carved spirals, diamonds, suns and other symbols indicates a ritual meaning to the sites. Many tombs are oriented in such a way as to allow the inner chamber to be illuminated by the rising sun on equinox or solstice days.

The early Irish had no cities, but lived in scattered family farmsteads throughout the countryside. Their dwellings consisted of ring forts, round enclosures encircled by earthen banks and built of wood or stone, and *crannogs*, which were platforms built on artificial islands in the lakes and enclosed by a wooden palisade. In the west, small stone *clochans*, or beehive huts, still dot the rocky hillsides.

Round towers

The early Christian era saw the birth of Ireland's most outstanding architecture. The tall, slim, round towers with their pointed caps are unique to Ireland and were built on monastic sites between 900 and 1200. Their Irish name, *cloigtheach*, means 'bell house', and they served as watch-towers and storehouses for manuscripts and treasures. The doors were built some 12ft (3.5m) from the ground and were reached by ladders which could be drawn up inside; thus they also served as refuges in times of attack. The monasteries also produced the exquisite carved stone high crosses that are the symbol of Ireland. From the 12th century, churches, previously unadorned, began to display carved ornamental decoration in the Romanesque style on doorways, windows and chancel arches; this was probably introduced by the English. Gothic architecture developed from the 13th century.

113

Castles and country seats

Irish castles, built by the gentry from the early 15th century, most frequently took the form of a fortified tower house, often surrounded by a bawn wall, which also protected residents of nearby farmsteads and livestock in times of danger. By contrast, the traditional Irish dwelling was a single-storey, rectangular cottage with one to three rooms and a thatched or slate roof.

Between 1714 and 1820 Georgian architecture reached its glory in neo-classical country manor houses such as Russborough House, Castle Coole and Emo Court. Dublin is known for the Georgian elegance of its red-brick, four-storey town houses, whose plain, well-proportioned façades are decorated with wrought-iron balconies, classical door frames and fanlights above the doors. These were generally built in terraces surrounding a central park or square. Towns such as Birr and Westport, with their tree-lined malls, also provide fine examples of Georgian design.

CORK AND KERRY

Cork and Kerry

From bustling Cork it is a short step to Ireland's southwestern corner, where the finger-like coastline reaches into the Atlantic, a land of hermits and saints, remote from the busy world.

BEST OF
Cork and Kerry

Getting there: Cork has a substantial airport (tel: 021 313131) served by flights from such UK airports as Stansted, Heathrow, Bristol, Birmingham, Manchester, Plymouth, Exeter and Newquay. There are also flights to Waterford airport from Stansted, Luton, and Manchester. Ireland's railway system will get you to Cork and Killarney but is not much help if you want to explore the headlands, cliffs and bays of the far southwest: a car is vital if you want to see some of Ireland's wildest and most romantic scenery.

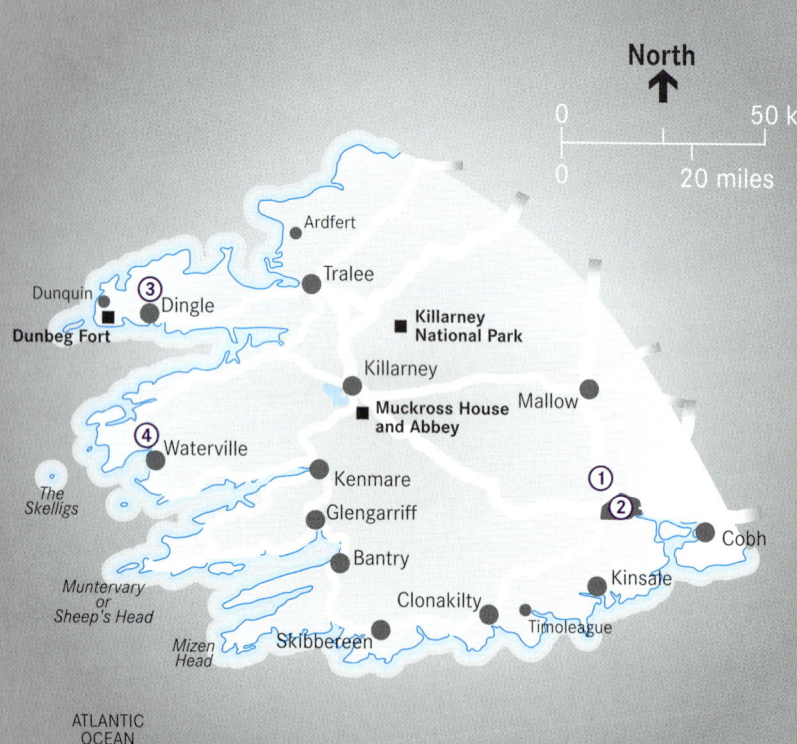

North

0   50 kr

0   20 miles

Ardfert

Dunquin   ③ Dingle
Tralee

Dunbeg Fort

■ Killarney
National Park

Killarney

■ **Muckross House**
and Abbey

Mallow

④ Waterville

The
Skelligs

Kenmare

Glengarriff
①

Bantry   ②   Cobh

Muntervary
or
Sheep's Head

Kinsale

Clonakilty

Skibbereen   Timoleague

Mizen
Head

ATLANTIC
OCEAN

① *Blarney*

Who in the world has not heard of the magical Blarney Stone, capable of conferring eloquence on even the most tongue-tied of visitors? Do you believe that? The only way you are going to find out if it's true is to try.
Pages 118–9

② *Cork*

Rebellious, artistic and bohemian, Cork is Ireland's second city, but only in terms of size and population. In every other respect the people of Cork see themselves as second to none, with their majestic buildings along the banks of the Lee and their lively French Quarter, Cork's answer to Dublin's Temple Bar, packed with chic boutiques, trendy bars, good value restaurants and fascinating craft shops. Pages 121–3

③ *The Dingle Peninsula*

Ireland's westernmost point is liberally sprinkled with prehistoric and early Christian remains – ogham stones, oratories, beehive huts and stone circles. Offshore, look out for Fungie the famous dolphin, swimming between the coastal islands and basking in Dingle harbour.
Pages 124–5

④ *The Ring of Kerry*

Fishing villages and captivating scenery make this circular route one of Ireland's most popular drives.
Pages 132–3

Tip

The Ring of Kerry, and to a lesser extent the Dingle Peninsula, are both very popular with coach tours and other drivers. Most tour coaches drive anti-clockwise. If you don't want your views to be blocked by the back end of a bus, you can either leave at the crack of dawn and endeavour to stay ahead of the coaches, or you can drive clockwise. In the latter case, you'll be battling these behemoths head-on round hairpin curves and on narrow roads that just aren't big enough for the both of you. If you spot an enormous red road hog bearing down upon you, brace yourself – some drivers have no qualms about taking your share of the tarmac.

Ardfert

Ardfert, north of Tralee, has the impressive ruins of a Romanesque cathedral and two churches dating from the 12th century, as well as remnants of a Franciscan friary. The nearby village of **Fenit** on Tralee Bay is said to be the birthplace of St Brendan the Navigator, who founded several monasteries and may have been one of the first Europeans to sail to America (*see page 138*). **Banna Strand**, to the northeast, is where Roger Casement was arrested trying to land rifles for the Easter Rising in 1916 (*see page 31*), and where David Lean shot the film *Ryan's Daughter* in 1970.

Bantry

Tourist Information Office: The Square. Tel: 027 50229. Seasonal opening.

This pleasant town with its broad square sits at the head of Bantry Bay. **Bantry House** (*tel: 027 50047; open: Apr–Oct 1000–1800; joint or separate ticket for the 1796 Bantry exhibition; ££*) enjoys a glorious setting, perched above the town amidst formal Italian gardens and terraces with sweeping vistas over the bay. The furnishings are as impressive as the drawing-room views: Gobelin and Aubusson tapestries, some made for Marie Antoinette's wedding to the Dauphin; huge Italian alabaster urns; early Waterford crystal chandeliers; and a peacock-blue dining-room with an ornately carved sideboard. Concerts are often held in the library.

Blarney

Whether or not you want to kiss the Blarney Stone and risk catching the gift of the gab, don't miss **Blarney Castle** (*tel: 021 385252; open: May and Sept 0900–1830; June–Aug, Mon–Sat 0900–1900; Oct–Apr 0900–sundown; Sun year round 0900–1730; ££*). It rises up amid wooded parkland, a glorious setting that doesn't fail to delight, in spite of the number of tourists who flock to one of Ireland's most popular castles. Built by Cormac MacCarthy in the 15th century, the fortress is a well-preserved ruin. There are wonderful panoramic views from the ramparts as you queue up to kiss the famous Stone. To achieve this feat, you must lie on your back and lean your head backwards into a crevasse, helped by a

guard and watched by the castle photographer who will capture this graceless moment for posterity. Afterwards, explore the pretty path that leads to the Rock Close, Druid circle and fairy glen – a truly enchanting spot.

Romancing the stone

The legend that the Blarney Stone imparts the gift of eloquence is a relatively recent one, thought to date from the late 18th century. Queen Elizabeth I made the name 'Blarney' synonymous with 'nonsense'. Her attempts to persuade Lord Blarney to bequeath his estate to the Crown were repeatedly met with elaborate excuses and fawning flattery. In exasperation she allegedly exclaimed: 'This is all Blarney! What he says he rarely means.'

Clonakilty

Tourist Information Office: Rossa Street. Tel: 023 33226. Open: July–Aug.

Clonakilty was founded in 1588 by the Great Earl of Cork, Richard Boyle. The **West Cork Regional Museum** (*Western Road; open: Mon–Sat; ££*) in the old schoolhouse traces the town's industrial past, while many buildings from that era along the quayside have been restored. The town is known for its traditional shopfronts with hand-painted signs, some of which sell the town's speciality, black puddings. The **West Cork Model Railway Village** (*Inchydoney Road; tel: 023 33224; open: Feb–Oct daily; ££*) portrays the town in the 1940s. The nearby Inchydoney beach is very popular. Also in the vicinity is the reconstructed Lisnagun Ring Fort.

Cobh

Cobh (pronounced 'cove') is situated on an island in Cork Harbour and joined to the mainland by a causeway. It was a quiet fishing village until the Napoleonic wars of the early 1800s, when the harbour flourished as a refuelling station for both naval and commercial ships. It later became an embarkation point for passenger vessels and the country's busiest port of emigration. In 1912 the *Titanic* made her last stop here before her fateful voyage.

The history of the town – and its temporary name change – is told in **The Queenstown Story** (*Cobh Heritage Centre; tel: 021 813591; open: daily 1000–1800; ££*), a multimedia exhibition housed in the Victorian Railway Station. **St Coleman's Cathedral**, a Gothic Revival edifice designed by Pugin in 1868, soars above the Victorian terraces lining the waterfront. Its carillon of 47 bells is the largest in Ireland. One-hour cruises on Cork Harbour are operated by **Marine Transport** from Cobh's Kennedy Pier (*tel: 021 811485; open: daily May–Sept; ££*).

Cork I

Tourist Information Office: Grand Parade. Tel: 021 273251. Open: Mon–Fri 0900–1800, Sat 0900–1300.

Cork is the Republic of Ireland's second largest city. Its Irish name, *corcaigh*, means 'marshy place', a reference to the estuary of the River Lee, where it grew up on islands in the 6th century. Its heart lies on an island still, formed by two channels of the river, and the many bridges give it a continental character. The city prospered from the butter trade in the 17th and 18th centuries, when many of the attractive Georgian buildings with their bowfront windows were built. Until around 1800, when the river was dammed, Patrick Street, the Grand Parade and other main streets were still under water. Cork's independent-minded citizenry gave only nominal obedience to the English crown. A hotbed of the nationalist Fenian movement, 'Rebel Cork' was burned in the War of Independence, 1919–21, but restoration in recent years has created a bright and attractive city with a lively nightlife and an acclaimed arts scene.

Cork II

*To see the city's highlights, start with the **English Market**, situated between the Grand Parade and Patrick Street, a covered food market dating from the early 17th century. Look for the ornate cast-iron fountain as you wander through, aiming for **Fitzgerald Park**, a delightful spot bordered to the north by the River Lee and to the south by the Mardyke, with its riverside walk.*

Housed in a Georgian mansion in the centre of the park is the **Cork Public Museum** (*tel: 021 270679; open: weekdays 1100–1300, 1415–1700, Sun 1500–1700; £*), which traces the social and political history of the town, including the conflicts of the 20th century.

Behind the Court House on Liberty Street, the **Cathedral of St Francis** is worth a visit to see its beautiful interior, with a sparkling mosaic reredos, domed ceiling, ornate archways and marble pillars. At the end of the street, continue straight

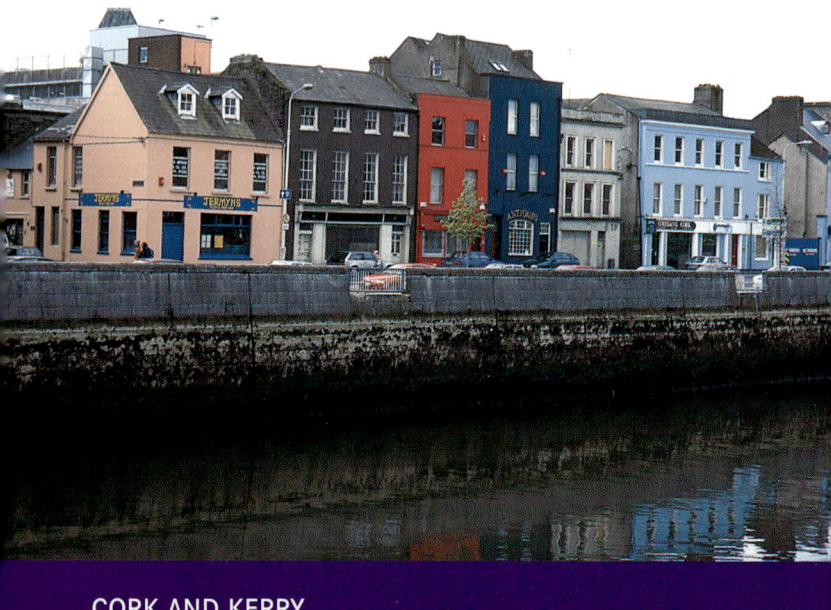

on along Castle and Paul streets. Off to the left is the **open-air flea market** on Corn Market Street. **Paul Street** is the heart of the old French Quarter, where Huguenots sought refuge from religious persecution. The piazza is a lively spot for buskers and street theatre, while the little side lanes, notably Carey's Lane and French Church Street, have interesting shops, bookshops and cafés.

Paul Street leads into Emmet Place, and the **Crawford Municipal Art Gallery** (*Emmet Place; tel: 021 273377; open: Mon–Sat 1000–1700; closed Sun; £*). The building itself is one of Cork's finest, built in 1724 of red brick dressed with limestone. Jack B Yeats, James Barry and Nathaniel Grogan are among the important Irish painters represented. The gallery café, run by the acclaimed Ballymaloe cookery school, is superb.

Cross over the bridge and continue straight ahead up the hill along John Street, turning left on John Redmond Street to reach **St Anne's Church** (*Church Street; open: May–Oct, Mon–Sat 0930–1700; Nov–Apr, 1000–1530; £*), where you can climb the 120-ft (36-m) tower and ring the bells, playing a tune with the help of 'music' cards. The clock face is known to locals as 'the four-faced liar' because each face showed slightly different times until it was repaired in 1986.

From the church, walk into the heart of the city along **St Patrick's Street**, which curves gracefully down to the Grand Parade. Cork's main thoroughfare is lined with Georgian buildings, their stately bowed windows overlooking the bustle of high-street shoppers. Follow pedestrianised **Cook Street** down to the South Mall: here large street-level gateways mark the presence of former boathouses, where merchants entered their warehouse by water. Cross over to the south side of the river, to Sullivan's Quay and French Quay, passing the ivy-laden **Elizabeth Fort**, built in the 16th century. Just beyond is **St Finbarre's Cathedral** (*Bishop Street; open: daily 0900–1800; £*). This triple-spired French Gothic cathedral, rich in sculptural decoration, was designed by William Burges and completed in 1878. Among its highlights are the west front, mosaic pavements, Bishop's Throne and the beautiful rose window.

The Dingle Peninsula

There's a touch of magic to the Dingle Peninsula. It stretches just 35 miles (56km) as the crow flies from Kerry's county town of Tralee to Slea Head, which looks out over the Blasket Islands, Ireland's 'last parish before America'. But within its bounds are rugged mountains, dramatic seascapes, idyllic beaches and steep slopes of the brightest green peppered with stone cottages, fences and curious beehive huts. The western half of the peninsula is a Gaeltacht area, a stalwart of traditional culture where Irish is the first language. It's no wonder the region is rich in Celtic legends.

Dingle, the peninsula's main town, is a lively place whose population doubles during the summer season (*Tourist Office: Main Street; tel: 066 51188 or 51241; seasonal opening*). The small streets winding up from the fishing harbour are lined with bright shops, good seafood restaurants and pubs renowned for their traditional music. In recent years, Dingle has become a hideaway haunt of Hollywood actors, who discovered its charms while filming in the area. The biggest star, however, is Fungie the bottlenose dolphin, who came to Dingle Bay in 1983 and made the harbour his home. Local boatmen at the quayside will take you out to see him, or you can don a wetsuit and join him for a swim.

Dunbeg Fort (*tel: 066 59070; freely accessible; ££*), clinging dramatically to the sheer black cliffs high above Dingle Bay, is one of the best preserved promontory forts remaining in Ireland. It dates from the Iron Age (500 BC–AD 500). With its inner stone rampart measuring over 20ft (6.35m) thick and some 10ft (3m) high, it was a defensive structure, rather than a homestead, and possibly served as a refuge for residents of the *clochans*, or beehive huts, that stood on the hillsides of Mount Eagle, behind the fort.

Dunquin, at the western end of the peninsula, was one of the locations used by David Lean for his film *Ryan's Daughter* (1970). The **Blasket Centre** here recounts the way of life of the Blasket Islanders, whose small population eked out a harsh living from fishing until 1953, when they were moved to the mainland. Boat trips to the islands can be arranged with local boatmen in the summer months; enquire at Dunquin Pier. Here you'll see upturned *curraghs* and the surrounding cliffs of colourful Silurian rock, over 400 million years old and rich in fossils.

The tip of the Dingle peninsula is littered with *clochans* – small stone **beehive huts** that were lived in by prehistoric people and hermits in the early Christian era. Some of the finest can be seen at Fahan, about a mile beyond Dunbeg Fort. One of Ireland's finest early Christian sites is **Gallarus Oratory,** a small church, built in the 7th or 8th century.

Its unusual shape, resembling an upturned boat, represents the height of an architectural technique known as corbelling, which was first developed by the builders of neolithic tombs. Unmortared stones, projecting inward and placed at an angle so that they were slightly lower on the outside, enabling rainwater to run off, were built up from both sides until they met at the top. The oratory has remained watertight for more than a thousand years.

Drombeg stone circle

The **Drombeg stone circle** lies 2 miles (3km) outside town via the R597 Glandore road. There are many stone circles in County Cork and this one, dating back to the 2nd century BC, is among the best preserved, with 17 standing stones forming a circle 30ft (9m) in diameter. Near by is a Stone Age cooking pit. There are also some sandy beaches and the ruins of Benduff Castle in the area.

Ogham stones

Ogham is an ancient system of writing, formed by combinations of lines and notches. The purpose of the stones appears to have been to mark territorial boundaries. Some 300 ogham stones have been found in Ireland, more than 80 of them in County Kerry alone. Once considered a pagan form of writing, recent studies date the stones to the 5th and 6th centuries, Ireland's early Christian era.

Glengarriff

Tourist Information Office: tel: 027 63084. Seasonal opening.

Sheltered beneath the Caha Mountains at the top of Bantry Bay, this village enjoys one of Ireland's finest settings. Its mild climate enables many Mediterranean plant species to flourish here, creating a lush landscape of flowers and foliage. It also contains one of the few remaining patches of the original oak forest which once covered the entire country. There are some beautiful woodland walks in **Glengarriff Forest Park**. Boat trips run throughout the day to **Garinish Island**, also called Ilnacullin, which is covered with luxuriant gardens (*tel: 027 63040; open: daily Mar–Oct; ££*). Created in 1910, its centrepiece is a formal Italianate garden, and the 37 acres (15 hectares) contain rock gardens, follies, pools and a host of exotic plants and shrubs. Watch for seals in the harbour on your way to and from the island.

Kenmare

Tourist Office and Kenmare Heritage Centre: The Square; tel: 064 41233. Open: Easter–Sept. ££.

Kenmare is a delightful heritage town with bright buildings, good shops and restaurants and traditional hand-painted signs. Its buildings and X-shaped street plan, which converges in a pleasant triangular square, date largely from the 18th century when it was part of the Landsdowne estate. The **Kenmare Heritage Centre**, at the tourist office, traces the town's history and has a walking trail around the town. Upstairs is the **Kenmare Lace and Design Centre** (*The Square; tel: 064 41491; £*), where you can see how the town's distinctive lace is made. The **Druid's Circle** is an impressive ring of 15 standing stones and a dolmen, located near the river off Market Street. **Seafari cruises** on the Kenmare River to see seals and other wildlife operate from Kenmare Pier. Cruises last 2 hours (*tel: 064 83171 for times and reservations*).

Kerry Way

The Kerry Way long-distance walking trail covers 134 miles (215km), beginning in Killarney National Park and continuing around the Iveragh peninsula. A booklet describing the route and a map guide are available from Cork Kerry Tourism. There are also several walks on Valencia Island. Kenmare holds walking festivals at Easter and Whitsuntide.

Killarney

Tourist Information Office: Town Centre Car Park, Beech Road. Tel: 064 31633; fax: 064 34506.

As the main tourist centre for the Ring of Kerry, Killarney is a busy town and often crowded, but once you're out of the car and on foot you can begin to appreciate its charms. A host of colourful little lanes, some still cobbled, run off the main streets. **St Mary's Cathedral**, designed by Pugin in the 1840s, is a splendid neo-Gothic Revival building with beautiful stained-glass windows. The Franciscan Friary and St Mary's Church of Ireland are also worth a visit. Killarney is known for its lively nightlife, ranging from traditional music and singing pubs to discos and cabarets. The town is particularly busy during the Killarney Rally in May, the Killarney Races in July and during the Easter folk festival.

Jaunting carts

Jaunting carts are a popular attraction around Killarney. These horse-and-traps can be hired for a spin around the grounds of Muckross House (see page 131), or for day-long sightseeing excursions, during which the 'jarveys' will fill your ears with local lore. Negotiate the price before you start the ride.

Killarney National Park

Killarney National Park covers 25 000 acres (10 000 hectares), encompassing the three lakes of Killarney and the surrounding mountains. It contains Ireland's largest area of natural oak woodlands, and the only remaining herd of native red deer. Among the many places of interest are **Ross Castle** on the shores of Lough Leane, **Innisfallen Island** with its ruined abbey, **Torc Waterfall**, and **Ladies' View**, with its superb vistas over the valley. A spectacular view of the lakes of Killarney can be had from **Aghadoe Hill**, north of the park on the Killarney–Tralee road. There are ruins of a round tower, castle and church. To the west of the park are the impressive peaks of **Macgillycuddy's Reeks**, which contain Ireland's highest mountain, **Carrantouhill**, rising 3 406ft (1 038m). The **Gap of Dunloe**, a glacier-carved pass, is a popular walking and horse-riding route, with dramatic views of deep gorges and lakes. It runs from **Kate Kearney's Cottage**, where 19th-century travellers stopped off for *poteen* (illegal liquor), to Moll's Gap.

Kinsale

Tourist Information Office: Pier Road; tel: 021 772234, fax: 021 774438. Open: Mar–Nov.

Kinsale is one of Ireland's most picturesque coastal towns. Set around a large harbour on the estuary of the River Bandon, it is filled with yachts and fishing boats and hosts international sailing events. Narrow streets lined with colourful, up-market shops, restaurants and pubs run back from the waterfront and up into the hills. Kinsale has become known as a gourmet capital, due to the quality of both the local seafood and the international chefs which the town attracts.

As you wander through town, look out for the **Old Courthouse**, now a regional museum; **St Multose Church**, dating from Norman times; and the ruins of **Desmond Castle**. Near by at Summer Cove is **Charles Fort** (*tel: 021 772263; open: daily Apr–Oct; ££*), a star-shaped bastion built around 1677 and in use until 1922. It has splendid views of Kinsale Harbour.

Mizen Head

Mizen Head is Ireland's most southwesterly point. The road from Schull runs along a dramatic rocky coastline, sliced by small coves and pounded by breaking waves, for 17 miles (27km) to these spectacular sandstone cliffs, which rise to over 755ft (230m). The views are fabulous, but the drops are sheer, so take care! The lighthouse here, built in 1910, was automated in 1993. Some of the buildings have been reopened as a visitor attraction; **Mizen Vision** (*tel: 028 35115; open: mid-Mar–May and Oct 1030–1700; June–Sept 1000–1800; Nov–Mar weekends only 1100–1400; ££*) has exhibits about the signal station and local lore. The road out to the point runs through the villages of Toormore and Goleen. **Crookhaven** is a delightful fishing and holiday village, a popular sailing centre. **Barleycove** is another popular small resort with a wonderful sandy beach.

Length and breadth

The phrase 'From Fair Head to Mizen Head' means the length and breadth of Ireland. It refers to Fair Head in County Antrim and Mizen Head in County Cork.

Muckross House and Abbey

Tel: 064 31440. House open: July–Aug, daily 0900–1900; Sept–June, daily 0900–1730; traditional farms open: mid-Mar–Apr, weekends 1400–1800; May, daily 1300–1800; June–Sept, daily 1000–1900; Oct, daily 1400–1800. Joint ticket available. ££.

There's a well-loved homely feel to this elegant, 19th-century Elizabethan-style mansion. You can imagine its residents relaxing around the exquisite inlaid games tables in the sitting room, which has fabulous views over Muckross Lake. In the basement of the house there are exhibits on stonework, bookbinding and traditional crafts. The gardens have beautiful displays of rhododendrons and azaleas, a water garden and a superb limestone rock garden. Also in the grounds are Muckross Traditional Farms, working farms that demonstrate the lifestyle and farming practices of Kerry countrymen in the 1930s, before the introduction of electricity.

The Ring of Kerry

The Ring of Kerry circles the Iveragh peninsula and is famous for its vistas of mountains and sea. This drive is the biggest draw in the west of Ireland, so don't expect to enjoy it in blissful solitude. Leave **Kenmare** *(see page* 127 *) on the N70, passing through* **Sneem** *and* **Caherdaniel***, where the road turns inland through a valley bordered by conifer-covered slopes and rugged mountains, then returns to the rocky coast with islands dotting the mint-coloured sea.*

At **Castlecove**, turn right at the signpost for **Staigue Fort**. Just beyond **Caherdaniel** is the turning for **Derrynane House**, the former home of Daniel O'Connell, 'The Liberator',

now a museum commemorating his life and political career (*tel: 066 75113; open: Apr and Oct, Tue–Sun 1300–1700; May–Sept, Mon–Sat 0900–1800, Sun 1100–1900; Nov–Mar, weekends 1300–1700; ££*).

There are stunning views over the ocean as the road climbs up the **Coomakesta Pass**. These are best enjoyed from the fine viewpoint beside the **Scarriff Inn**. You then descend to **Waterville**, set low on the shores of Ballinskelligs Bay, a popular resort. The main road now cuts inland across the peninsula to **Cahersiveen**.

Just beyond Waterville, the R567 to the left leads to **Ballinskelligs**, a Gaeltacht village with the ruins of an ancient castle and abbey, and a magnificent sandy beach stretching for 4 miles (6km). Also off the N70, the R565 runs to Portmagee and the land bridge to **Valencia Island**. This lush, scenic island is a departure point for boat trips to the **Skelligs**, which can be seen offshore (*see page 134*).

The N70 north from **Cahersiveen** is one of the finest stretches of the Ring, with superb views across Dingle Bay to the peaks of the **Slieve Mish Mountains**. The road hugs the coast, then climbs into the rugged mountains before dropping down again into **Glenbeigh**. This small village, a good base for hiking and fishing, is built on a seaside bog. The **Kerry Bog Village Museum** (*tel: 066 72777; open: Mar–May and Oct, weekdays 0930–1730; June–Sept, Mon–Sat 1000–1800, Sun 1400–1800; ££*), beside the Red Fox Inn, re-creates life here in the early 1800s. The **Tower Old Bar**, on Main Street in Glenbeigh, is an atmospheric spot for a drink, with low ceilings and old stone walls, and a big, warm open fire. Near by at **Rossbeigh** there is a beautiful strand backed by high dunes.

Killorglin, 6 miles (10km) on, is a pleasant town, famous for its Puck Fair in August, when a large goat is crowned King of the Fair. From here it is 13 miles (21km) to **Killarney** (*see page 128*) on the N72. Follow the N71 along Lough Leane to Muckross. Here you can tour lovely **Muckross House and Abbey** (*see page 131*). The N71 continues on through Moll's Gap back to Kenmare.

Sheep's Head Peninsula

This long, narrow peninsula runs between Bantry Bay and Dunmanus Bay for 15 miles (24km) to its tip at Muntervary, or Sheep's Head. It is the least visited of Cork's southwestern peninsulas, with a rugged rocky landscape and beautiful views of the rocky outcrops and tiny offshore islands. At **Akahista** there are good sandy beaches and a memorial to those who died when an Air India plane crashed offshore in 1985. At the main village of **Kilcrohane** there is another good beach. Intrepid explorers can continue straight on across a rather desolate stretch to a car park, where a footpath leads to land's end at the **Sheep's Head**. Most follow the scenic **Goat's Path Road**, signposted at Kilcrohane, which crosses the peninsula, climbing up into the mountains along Seefin, the highest peak.

The Skelligs

The Skelligs is a group of three conical rock islands lying about 9 miles (14km) off Valencia Island, where the **Skellig Experience** (*tel: 066 76306; open: Mar–Oct, daily 1000–1800; ££*) tells the story of the islands' heritage and wildlife. Cruises to the Skelligs operate from alongside. The largest island is **Skellig Michael**, rising more than 700ft (213m) out of the sea. Early Christian monks built a settlement of beehive huts, oratories and two churches atop the rock. **Little Skellig**, like its bigger brother, has steep cliffs that are home to breeding colonies of gannets, puffins, storm petrels and other seabirds.

Timoleague

The ruins of an early 14th-century Franciscan abbey at Timoleague enjoy a romantic waterside setting overlooking Courtmacsherry Bay. Near by, **Timoleague Castle Gardens** (*tel: 023 46116; open: Easter weekend and June–Aug, daily 1200–1800; ££*) were laid out from 1820 on the grounds of a 13th-century castle, little of which remains.

Tralee

Tourist Information Office: Ashe Memorial Hall, Denny Street. Tel: 066 21288. Open: all year.

The capital of County Kerry was made famous years ago by the old Irish ballad, *The Rose of Tralee*. **Kerry the Kingdom** (*Ashe Memorial Hall, Denny Street; tel: 066 27777; open: mid-Mar–Dec, daily 1000–1800; 'til 1900 in Aug*) tells the county's history from prehistoric times in three combined attractions: the audio-visual show gives an overview of Kerry's sights and scenery; the Kerry County Museum uses modern interpretative media alongside the artefacts and displays; and the Geraldine Tralee is a time-travel ride through the sights, sounds and smells of medieval Tralee.

The **Tralee and Dingle Steam Railway** (*tel: 066 21064 or 28888; departures on the hour from Ballyard Station in Tralee and on the half hour from Blennerville; open: May–Sept 1100–1730 and holiday periods; £££*) is a popular excursion. It runs for 3 miles (5km) to the **Blennerville Windmill** (*tel: 066 21064; open: daily Apr- Oct; ££*), which has been turned into a visitor centre with interesting activities and exhibits.

The *Jeannie Johnson* was a remarkable 19th-century vessel that transported thousands of emigrants to North America and never lost a single passenger to accident or disease. A full-size replica is now being built at the **Jeannie Johnson Shipyard** in Blennerville which will retrace the Atlantic voyage (*tel: 066 27777 for opening times*).

Eating and drinking

Bantry

O'Connor's Seafood Restaurant
Main Street. Tel: 027 50221. ££–£££. Mussels are the speciality at this cosy restaurant, which also features daily seafood specials, live lobsters, steaks and oysters from a sea-water tank. Lighter meals are served in the back bar.

Cork

The **Gingerbread House** on Paul Street is a great stop for coffee or lunch. It serves delicious sandwiches, baguettes and irresistible homemade cakes, desserts and ice cream.

Dunquin

Dunquin Pottery and Café
Slea Head Road. Tel: 066 56194. £. Known for its distinctive hand-thrown stoneware, the café serves homemade soups, savouries and baked goods.

Kenmare

Micky Ned's
6 Henry Street. Tel: 064 41591. £. This charming coffee shop and deli serves homemade soups, sandwiches, salads, quiche and the best apple crumble in the world! Great coffee and a delicious selection of home-baked goods make this a good refuge on a rainy day, or take away some paté, smoked salmon and Irish cheeses for a picnic on the Ring.

Killarney

Muckross Park Hotel
Muckross Village. Tel: 064 31938; fax: 064 31965. ££–£££. Beautifully situated in Killarney National Park, opposite the grounds of Muckross Abbey, Killarney's oldest hotel dates from 1795. The Bluepool Restaurant, overlooking landscaped gardens that lead down to the river, has innovative cuisine and fine wines. Adjoining the hotel is Molly Darcy's, a large, lively pub and restaurant, with stone walls, beamed ceilings, open fires and traditional music.

Kinsale

The White House
Market Square. Tel: 021 772125. £–£££. Whatever your budget, you can sample Kinsale's outstanding cuisine at one of two restaurants in this town-centre hotel. Chelsea's is an informal bistro adjoining the lively pub. It does a fantastic seafood chowder served with homebaked brown bread, as well as steaks, salads and pasta dishes. Le Restaurant d'Antibes, a member of the Kinsale Good Food Circle, which is a hallmark of quality, has fine dining in an intimate setting. Prime meats, poultry and fresh local seafood are prepared and served with flair.

The Spaniard Inn
Scilly. Tel: 021 772436. £. This atmospheric pub, in a long yellow building perched on a hillside opposite the town centre, has log walls, low ceilings, an open fire and sawdust-covered floors. A favourite haunt of local fishermen, it often has traditional music. There is also a restaurant.

Mizen Head

O'Sullivan's Pub, opposite the pier at Crookhaven, is a charming spot, with an open fire for cold, wet days and outdoor picnic tables for sunny ones. It's a popular gathering spot and serves chowder, soups, sandwiches and desserts.

Festivals

Bantry is the site of Murphy's International Mussel Fair, held in early May, a long weekend of music, dancing, street entertainment, cooking competitions and, of course, mussels from Bantry Bay.

Tralee holds a festival of the same name every August, in which women from Irish communities around the world compete for the title of Rose of Tralee. Music, dancing, parades and a horse race also mark the event. The National Folk Theatre of Ireland, Siamsa Tíre, is based here, and there are performances of traditional music and dance throughout the summer.

Shopping

The major high-street chains can be found in Cork along Patrick Street. Roches Department Store is the largest in town, while Cash's, next door, carries more up-market fashions. At the top of the street, near the bridge, is a huge shopping complex at Merchant's Quay. The English Market, off Princes Street and the Grand Parade, sells a wonderful variety of foodstuffs, from Irish farm cheeses, smoked salmon, fruit and veg to more acquired specialities such as tripe and blood sausage. The shops in the old French Quarter around Paul Street are noted for modern Irish crafts and design, and you'll also find a string of antiques shops in Paul's Lane. Bargain hunters may enjoy the open-air flea market on Corn Market Street, also called Coal Quay.

Entertainment

Dingle

In a town known for its traditional music, one name that always pops up is O'Flaherty's (UaFlaibeartaig), on Bridge Street, near the town entrance. Its simple, rustic interior is the scene of impromptu *seisuns* (music sessions) on most summer nights.

Dunquin

This Dingle Peninsula town boasts the most westerly pub in Europe. Kruger's offers sessions and set dancing, and is named after the local hero, the late Kruger Kavanagh, who was a soldier, impresario, storyteller, political activist and bodyguard to Eamon de Valera.

Visionaries and emigrants

Rising to 3127ft (953m), Mount Brandon, on the Dingle Peninsula, has been a holy mountain since ancient times. The mountain top was the site of the harvest festival of Lughnasa, dedicated to the Celtic god Lugh. Like most other pagan sites, it was then appropriated by an early Christian saint. In this case it was St Brendan, who built a hermitage here in the 6th century – and then a remarkable thing happened: Brendan experienced a vision on top of the mountain in which he saw a land called Hy-Brasil, the promised land.

The voyage of St Brendan

The vision inspired Brendan to gather together a group of Irish monks who made a great sea voyage, which may have taken them to the New World, long before the Vikings or Columbus made the same trip. According to a medieval manuscript, the *Navigato Brendan*, Brendan and his band set sail in hide-covered *curraghs* across the Atlantic in search of the land he had seen in his vision. During their seven-year odyssey they encountered fire-hurtling demons, a floating crystal column and a sea creature as large as an island. Could these have been a volcanic eruption on Iceland, an iceberg and a whale? If the utopian world that Brendan duly reached was indeed North America, no archaeological proof has been found – yet many medieval explorers believed Brendan's tale, and place-names from the saga appear on some medieval maps and charts. Tim Severin, the English explorer, built a replica of St Brendan's boat and successfully retraced the epic voyage in 1976, proving that it was at least a possibility that the Irish could have been the first Europeans to reach the New World (the boat used in the voyage can be seen at Craggaunowen – *see page 147*).

Irish emigration

Between 1848 and 1950 more than six million people followed in Brendan's footsteps and emigrated from Ireland to America. Around 2^1/$_2$ million – well over a third – departed from Cobh. The exodus began in the famine years (1845–50), when 1^1/$_2$ million left – nearly one-fifth of the pre-famine population. The United States and Canada were the primary destinations, though some ventured further to Australia. This traumatic and desperate flight was the largest single population movement of the 19th century. Health and sanitary conditions on the 'coffin ships' were appalling, and in 1847 alone, 40 000 died at sea or in Canadian quarantine stations. Most emigrants were farmers or labourers, and the cost of the passage was greater than their annual income. As the famine worsened, many landlords found it cheaper to provide assisted passages to their poverty-stricken tenants than to support them at home. Emigration was seen as the solution to Ireland's main social problem: the burgeoning population of landless poor.

Shannonside and The Burren

The Shannon region is brimming with castles, some in ruins, others restored as hotels and medieval banquet halls. There are also archaeological sites, picturesque villages such as Adare, and the fine reconstructions of Celtic life at Craggaunowen. Not far away is one of Ireland's most fascinating landscapes, the sweeping limestone plateau known as The Burren. It stretches for miles inland from the Atlantic, with rare and delicate wild flowers adding splashes of colour to its grey canvas.

141

SHANNONSIDE AND THE BURREN

BEST OF

Shannonside and The Burren

Getting there: Shannon airport (tel: 061 471444) is served by flights from other Irish cities and from the UK, and there is a bus service taking passengers onwards from the airport to Ennis and Limerick. Both towns are also served by Ireland's railway system, but, as always in Ireland, you will need a car if you want to explore the Burren and points west.

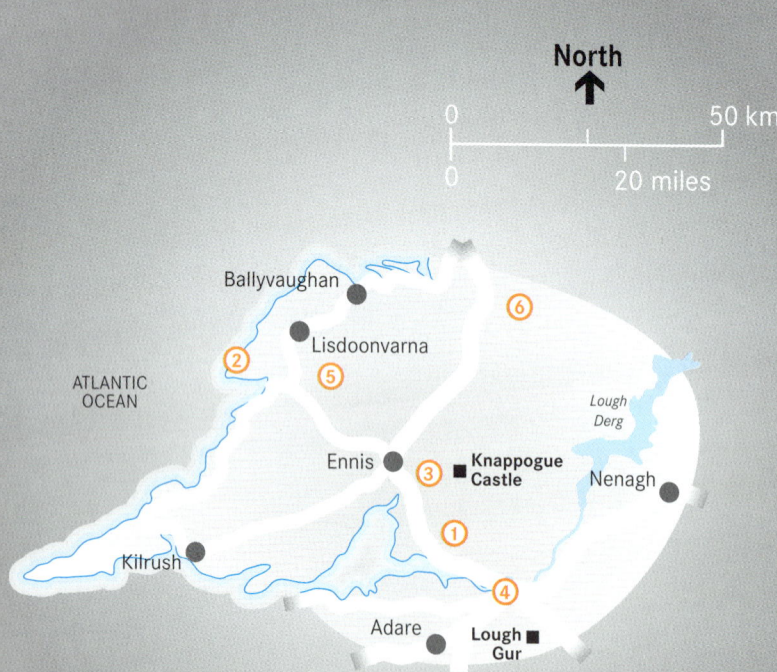

North

| 0 | | 50 km |
| 0 | 20 miles | |

ATLANTIC OCEAN

Ballyvaughan

Lisdoonvarna ⑤

②

Ennis ③ ■ Knappogue Castle

Nenagh

Lough Derg

①

⑥

Kilrush

Adare ④ ■ Lough Gur

① Bunratty Castle and Folk Park

It's easy to knock the cod medievalism of this tourist attraction, with its popular mead and chicken-leg banquets, but there is much that is good and authentic here as well, including reconstructions of the furnishings and appearance of the castle in its heyday. **Page 145**

② Cliffs of Moher

Vertigo sufferers beware: these are among Europe's tallest sea cliffs – guaranteed to set your head awhirl – unless you are a seabird, in which case you will recognise this as one of Europe's most densely populated high-rise nesting sites. **Page 146**

③ Craggaunowen

Was St Brendan the first European to visit America, or was it all a bad dream? Visit Craggaunowen to learn about Tim Severin's journey across the Atlantic in the footsteps of the early Christian monk, and enjoy history demonstrations which highlight the life of Ireland's early Iron Age inhabitants. **Page 147**

④ Limerick

Ireland's fourth-largest city was the setting for Frank McCourt's prize-winning *Angela's Ashes*, and you can tour the places that he wrote about in his semi-autobiographical work. **Page 148**

⑤ Kilfenora and The Burren

Come to Kilfenora's Burren Centre before heading off to explore this botanist's paradise, famed for its rare blue gentians, rock roses, mountain avens and 22 varieties of orchid. **Pages 150–1**

⑥ Thoor Ballylee

Lovers of Yeats' poetry will enjoy visiting the atmospheric tower that served as the poet's summer home and inspired some of his most lyrical verse. The audio-visual programme gives an introduction to the man and the influences on his work. There is a magnificent view of the surrounding countryside from the top of the tower and a pretty walk beside the stream to a restored mill race. **Page 151**

143

Adare

Tourist Information Office: Adare Heritage Centre. Tel: 061 396666; fax: 061 396932. The office offers guided walking tours of the town's historical highlights.

People come to Adare to see the row of charming thatched cottages, several of which now house restaurants and craft shops, along its busy main street. With up-market modern homes spreading out from the centre, Adare is hardly the quaint village you would expect, but the stone buildings and ruins are highly attractive and well worth a visit. The **Adare Heritage Centre**, which contains the tourist office and knitwear and craft shops, presents a historical exhibition on the town. Next door is the **Trinitarian Monastery**, founded in the 1230s, and now incorporated into the Catholic church. The order was established in France to rescue hostages taken during the Crusades, and this was the only known branch in Ireland. Across the River Maigue are the ruins of **Desmond Castle**. Near by, a short walk across the golf course, are the ruins of the **Franciscan Friary**.

Ballyvaughan

This attractive fishing village is a popular spot for holidaymakers renting its whitewashed thatched cottages, as well as for day-trippers from around the region. On a sunny weekend you may encounter a small traffic jam as everyone vies for a parking spot near the popular Monk's Pub. There are boat trips from the harbour to the Aran Islands, and a number of good craft shops. Just outside town is the **Aillwee Cave** (*tel: 065 77036; open: mid-Mar–Nov, daily 1000–1730 (1830 July–Aug); ££*), a vast cavern formed more than two million years ago by an underground river, full of fantastic formations and a waterfall. You can see the cave on a 30-minute guided tour. There is a warren of caves throughout the Burren, but this is the only one accessible to the public.

Bunratty Castle and Folk Park

Tel: 061 361511. Open: June–Aug, daily 0930–1900, Sept–May, daily 0930–1730; last admission to castle 1600. £££.

One of Ireland's most popular castles, Bunratty Castle was built in 1425, though its origins date back to Viking times. It has been restored to its medieval glory and filled with a superb collection of medieval furniture that greatly enhances its atmosphere. Highlights include the great hall with its timbered roof and tapestries, the 'murder holes' through which enemies were drenched in boiling oil, and the banqueting hall, where the popular medieval banquets take place. Surrounding the castle is the delightful Folk Park, where there are re-creations of a village street, fisherman's cottage, farmhouses, a forge and other period buildings that illustrate all walks of life in days gone by.

Cliffs of Moher

Tel: 065 81565. Open: May–June, 0900–1830; July–Aug, 0900–2100; Sept–Apr, 0930–1800. Parking ££.

These sheer striated cliffs, rising over 700ft (215m) out of the Atlantic, are one of the west coast's most impressive natural sights. Stretching for nearly 5 miles (8km) along the coast, they form a massive housing estate for nesting gulls, kittiwakes, puffins and other seabirds. **O'Brien's Tower**, built in the 19th century as a viewpoint for Victorian tourists, sits atop the highest cliff; on a clear day you can see the mountains of Connemara. Regrettably, the site is spoiled by its own popularity. Beggars, buskers and cassette vendors lend it all the atmosphere of a carnival pier. The best way to experience the cliffs is to set off on the path to Hag's Head, about an hour south; a walking guide can be purchased in the visitor centre.

Craggaunowen

Tel: 061 367178. Open: mid-Mar–Oct, daily 1000–1800 (last admission 1700). ££.

Craggaunowen was the brainchild of the late John Hunt, who, having restored the 16th-century castle, set about reconstructing dwellings that portray the lifestyle of the ancient Celts. A fine *crannog*, or lake dwelling, a ring fort and a hunter's cooking site are set along a woodland trail. The Iron Age field and the *togher* – a relic of an ancient wooden roadway built across a bog – provide insight into how they survived. A fascinating piece of recent history is *The Brendan*, the leather-hulled boat in which Tim Severin crossed the Atlantic in 1976 in an effort to authenticate the voyage of St Brendan the Navigator (*see page 138*).

Ennis

Tourist Information Office: Clare Road. Tel: 065 28366. Open: all year. It produces a walking trail to sights of interest in the town.

Clare's county town dates from 1240 when the O'Briens, kings of Thomond, invited the Franciscans to establish a settlement on an island, or 'Inis', formed by two streams of the River Fergus. The **Friary** (*Abbey Street; tel: 065 29100; open: mid-Apr–Sept 0930–1830; other times by arrangement; ££*) still stands and is famous for its richly carved monuments, particularly the 15th-century McMahon tomb. The town is a lively and characterful place, with narrow winding streets and bright shopfronts in the town centre. Numerous mementoes from Irish political history can be seen in the **Ennis Museum**.

Knappogue Castle

Tel: 061 368103. Open: Apr–Oct 0930–1730; last admission 1630. ££.

Knappogue Castle, built in 1467, is a typical example of the type of fortified tower house favoured by the Irish and Anglo-Irish ruling class. The tower consists of four storeys connected by a spiral staircase. The upper floors were used as living and sleeping quarters, with the lord of the castle residing at the top. The ground floor was primarily used for storage. Today it houses the banquet hall, where Knappogue's medieval banquets take place (*see page 152*).

Limerick

Tourist Information Office: Arthur's Quay. Tel: 061 317522; fax: 061 317939.

The Republic's fourth-largest city shot to fame in 1996 as the setting for Frank McCourt's memoir *Angela's Ashes*. While some natives take issue with his portrayal of their city, it has none the less sparked visitor interest. The slums of McCourt's childhood have long gone, and Limerick's beautifully renovated Georgian buildings – best seen along the Crescent and O'Connell Street – and its prosperous city centre create a fine impression of the city today.

With its strategic location on the Shannon, Limerick dates back to Celtic times. In its long and often turbulent history it has been settled by the Vikings, walled and segregated by the English, and defended by Irish patriots against Cromwell and during the Jacobite wars.

Limerick's attractions include the **Hunt Museum** (*Custom House, Rutland Street; tel: 061 312833; open: Tue–Sun; ££*), with a superb collection of Celtic and medieval treasures as well as Irish and European paintings, and the **Limerick Museum** (*St John's Square; tel: 061 417826; open: Tue–Sat; £*), which also has a fine collection of artefacts, including a brass-topped stone pillar known as 'the Nail'; this is where business transactions were finalised with cash 'on the Nail'.

In the old medieval city **St Mary's Cathedral** (*Bridge Street; open: daily in summer 0900–1300, 1400–1700; £*) dates from the 12th century and has interesting tombs, while **King John's Castle** (*tel: 061 361511; open: Apr–Oct, daily 0930–1730; last admission 1630; Nov–Mar, weekends 0930–1730; ££*) is a Norman fortress that houses good historical exhibitions. Alongside the castle is **Castle Lane**, an authentic 18th- to 19th-century streetscape. Whether or not you're a McCourt fan, pay a visit to **Mungret Abbey**, where Angela's ashes were finally scattered in the churchyard. These atmospheric ruins lie on the southwestern outskirts of town and date back to the 6th century.

Lisdoonvarna

Lisdoonvarna is a Victorian spa town, and the sulphurous waters are still the main attraction today. You can have a sulphur bath, massage and other treatments at the **Spa Wells Health Centre** (*tel: 065 74023; open: June–mid-Oct, daily 1000–1800; book in advance*), a complex set in parkland on the edge of town, and Ireland's only working spa. The town's other claim to fame is its Matchmaking Festival, held in late September, a traditional gathering spot for bachelor farmers in search of a wife.

Tours

The tourist office has devised two walking tours (Limerick – the Past Revisited *) which highlight the many places of interest; or you can see the sights on two open-top bus tours, one covering medieval and Georgian Limerick, the other visiting the settings in McCourt's memoir. Contact Bus Eireann (* tel: 061 313333 *).*

Lough Gur

Tel: 061 360788. Open: May–Sept, 1000–1800. ££.

The remains of one of Ireland's earliest settlements are scattered around Lough Gur, an idyllic lake in the Limerick countryside. Gold and bronze objects, plus spearheads and shields found in the water indicate that the lake was a sacred site well into Christian times. The Lough Gur wedge tomb can be seen along the road that leads to the visitor centre, which traces the history of the site in detail. This communal grave, dated to around 2500 BC, was a ritual site and Early Bronze Age beakerware pottery was found here.

Kilfenora and The Burren

Comprising only 13 parishes, Kilfenora is the smallest Catholic diocese in Ireland, yet by some hierarchical twist it has none other than the pope as bishop! The village is known as the 'City of the Crosses' because of the fine high crosses that adorn the grounds of its ruined 12th-century cathedral — the **Doorty Cross** near the door and the **West Cross** or 'Cross in the Field' are among the finest to survive.

Kilfenora is also home to the **Burren Centre** (*tel: 065 88030; open: mid-Mar–Oct, daily; ££*), which contains excellent models and exhibits explaining the geology, flora and fauna of this unique landscape. The Burren, a sweeping area of rocky hills and plateaux covering 62 square miles (161 sq km), is covered by a huge limestone pavement, consisting of 'clints', which are broken by vertical fissures called 'grikes'. These have allowed the rainwater to drain through and carve out an extensive system of underground caves.

At first glance these vast fields of grey seem lonely and desolate. On closer inspection, splashes of colour appear between the crevices. The Burren is a **botanist's paradise**, for the microclimate here nurtures an amazing number of rare plant species, including alpine and Mediterranean varieties seldom found in Ireland. Among the blue gentians, rock roses and mountain avens are 22 varieties of orchid. The flowers in turn attract some 28 species of butterfly. May through to August is the best time to see this floral display.

Thoor Ballylee

Tel: 091 631436. Open: Easter–Sept, daily 1000–1800. ££.

This abandoned 14th-century fortified tower was the summer home of the poet William Butler Yeats from 1916. He wrote much poetry here, including *The Winding Stair* and *The Tower*. It has been restored to look as it did when the Yeats family lived here, and the self-guided tour can be enhanced by an audio reading of Yeats' works. **Coole Park** (*tel: 091 631804; open: daily 1000–dusk; visitor centre open: mid-Apr–mid-June and Sept, Tue–Sat 1000–1700; mid-June–Aug, daily 0930–1830; ££*), the home of Yeats' patron, Lady Gregory, is 4 miles (6km) away. The house is gone and the grounds are now a national park, but you can still see the Autograph Tree where many famous literary figures carved their initials.

Eating and drinking

Ballyvaughan

Monk's Bar and Seafood Restaurant

Tel: 065 707 7059. £. Seafood is the speciality at this popular bar, located on the main road near the pier. The chowder is great, and so is the atmosphere.

Ennis

Cloister

Abbey Street. Tel: 065 682 9521. ££. This restaurant is set in a beautifully furnished period building in the shadow of the old Franciscan abbey. The three-course menu includes oysters, wild Atlantic mussels, meat, fish and vegetarian dishes. There is also casual dining in the Friary Bar during the day.

Epicerie du Centre

O'Connell Street. Tel: 065 43577. Closed Sun. £. Elizabeth David would have approved – a wine bar selling the simplest of foods: an omelette, a plate of sausage, a selection of cheese – all chosen to complement the wines.

Fawl's Pub

O'Connell Street, across from the cathedral. This is an authentic Irish pub with a small front bar and a large beer garden at the back, where set dances sometimes take place.

Limerick

Green Onion

Rutland Street. Tel: 061 400710. Closed Sun. ££. Opposite the Hunt Museum, Green Onion is Limerick's favourite eating spot, abuzz with people coming and going at all times of the day. Even so, the old wooden booths give you privacy if that's your desire. The food ranges from full Irish breakfast to such eclectic dishes as jerk chicken with jalapeno salsa or a lentil and bacon casserole made with best Puy lentils.

Medieval banquets

If quaffing mead and feasting on roast beast in a genuine medieval dining hall strikes your fancy, you've come to the right region. Bunratty Castle, Knappogue Castle and Dunguaire Castle at Kinvara hold medieval banquets twice nightly in season (year-round at Bunratty). These royal repasts are accompanied by music, entertainment and merry-making. Bunratty also holds Traditional Irish Nights in the Great Barn. For information contact Shannon Castle Banquets (tel: 061 360788 *) or local tourist offices.*

Shopping

Ardara

There are several factory outlet shops selling hand-loomed sweaters and knitwear, tweed jackets and other goods. These include **John Molloy**, on the outskirts of town, **Bonners**, **Kennedy's** and **Triona Design**.

Ennis

Custy's Traditional Music Shop
Francis Street (off Abbey Street near Queen's Hotel). Tel: 065 682 1727.
A charming little shop with a good selection of traditional music and instruments including bodhráns, fiddles and flutes.

Picnic at Aillwee Cave

Ballyvaughan is a good place to stock up for a picnic, because the shop at Aillwee Cave is an unexpected source of good local food, including the award-winning local cheeses Burren Gold, similar to an aged Gouda, with the same rich nutty flavour.

Entertainment

Among the many pubs in **Ennis** where you can hear traditional music, one of the best known is **Cruise's Pub and Restaurant**, next to the friary in Abbey Street. Sessions are often held in **The Sanctuary**, decorated to look like a medieval castle (*tel: 065 41800*). Ennis is also famous for traditional music and hosts the annual **Fleadh Nua** music festival at the end of May.

Irish eloquence

Irish poetry and stories, like the Irish soul, are forever linked to the land. A love of nature – and an awareness of mankind's place in it – is ever-present and imbues the spirit of Irish eloquence.

Mythology

Ireland is rich in folklore and mythology, from the fairy people to the Celtic gods and heroes. Reading just a few of these tales will add greatly to the atmosphere of any journey through Ireland.

The fairy people, who are said to be fallen angels, redundant gods or an ancient race lost in the mists of time, make love, war and beautiful music. Their most famous member is the leprechaun, a grouchy old shoemaker, who buries the riches of his trade at the end of the rainbow. Numerous customs have sprung from the need to placate the fairies; for example, ash was placed on the threshold to protect an unattended child in a cradle from fairy abductions.

Literature

Classic Irish literature includes poetry by W B Yeats and Louis MacNeice; *Dubliners*, *Ulysses* and *Finnegans Wake* by James Joyce; *Waiting for Godot* by the playwright Samuel Beckett; and short stories by Frank O'Connor, Elizabeth Bowen and Sean O'Faolain. Anthologies such as *The Field Day Anthology of Irish Writing*, a three-volume tome edited by Seamus Dean, and collections of Irish verse provide an overview of the wealth of talent.

Works by J M Synge are wonderfully evocative of Irish life in the early 1900s. Bernadette Devlin's *The Price of My Soul* and Dervla Murphy's *A Place Apart* give heartfelt insights into Northern Ireland.

In 1996 poet Seamus Heaney became the fourth Irish winner of the Nobel Prize for Literature. Contemporary Irish works include Roddy Doyle's *The Van* and *Paddy Clark Ha Ha Ha* and Frank McCourt's memoir *Angela's Ashes*.

Will o' the Wisp

Strange glowing lights can sometimes be seen on Irish bogs at night. Some say it is Jack O'Lantern, a shoemaker who was condemned to wander the bogs for murdering a child. Such lights can cause a person to stray from the path and fall into a bog hole. To ward off this evil, people are advised to turn their coats inside out immediately on sighting the Will o' the Wisp.

The west
of Ireland

Ireland's west is home to thousands of native Gaelic speakers, so Irish traditions hold sway, including traditional music and Irish-language theatre. The west also embraces some of Ireland's wildest and most beautiful areas, from the wilderness of Connemara National Park to the remote Aran Islands.

THE WEST OF IRELAND

BEST OF
The west of Ireland

Getting there: every road in the west is a scenic one, and there is much to explore, but you will need your own transport, because much of Ireland's western expanse is otherwise inaccessible. The train will take you as far as Galway City, and then you are on your own. Knock International airport (tel: 094 67222) has flights from Dublin, Stansted and Manchester.

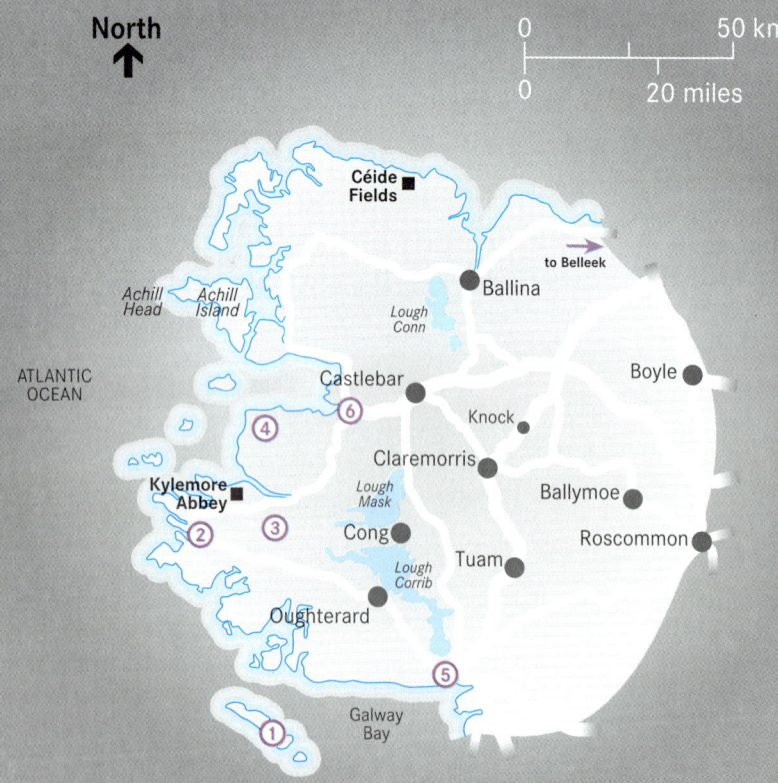

North

0   50 km
0   20 miles

Céide Fields

to Belleek

Ballina

Lough Conn

Achill Head

Achill Island

ATLANTIC OCEAN

Castlebar

(6)

(4)

Boyle

Knock

Claremorris

Lough Mask

Kylemore Abbey

(2)

(3)

Cong

Lough Corrib

Tuam

Ballymoe

Roscommon

Oughterard

(5)

(1)

Galway Bay

① *Aran Islands*

Hire a bicycle or jump into a jaunting car to explore Inishmore, the largest of the three Aran islands. As well as glorious beaches, the islands are covered in important prehistoric and early Christian remains, from the ruins of the Dun Aengus Bronze Age fort, to the ruins of St Enda's 5th-century monastery. **Page 161**

② *Clifden*

Founded as a 'pocket of respectability amidst the lawlessness of Connemara', Clifden is a beautiful town of craft shops and lively pubs famous for their music, with a skiline dominated by the twin spires of its two churches. **Page 163**

③ *Connemara National Park*

Life was a struggle in boggy Connemara, one of Ireland's poorest regions, but the wildlife is thriving and there is fascinating ecology to explore if you join one of the visitor centre's guided walks. Wild ponies graze fields that are hedged with fuchsia bushes, just one of many plants that thrive in the mild westerly climate. **Page 164**

④ *Croagh Patrick*

County Mayo's holy mountain has been sacred to Christians since St Patrick colonised the peak by fasting here for 40 days and 40 nights in AD 441 – but the mountain's Christian heritage is as nothing compared to the 5 000 years that the mountain has been at the centre of pagan worship and myth. **Page 165**

⑤ *Galway*

Galway's star is rising as a great place to live and work, with some of Ireland's best restaurants, pubs and shops, and the beautiful west coast on its doorstep. Come here to see what the fuss is about and maybe you will be reluctant to leave. **Pages 166-9**

⑥ *Westport*

Leafy Westport is a planned town, and the work of no less an architect than James Wyatt, the English-born architect and contemporary of Robert Adam. See his elegant townscapes and visit the imposing country house that he designed for the Earls of Altamont, with its theatrical staircase and elegant rooms. **Page 171**

159

Achill Island

Tourist Information Office: The Sound. Tel: 098 45384. Open: late May–Aug, Mon–Sat 1000–1730.

At 15 miles (24km) long and 12 miles (19km) wide, Achill is Ireland's largest island. It has splendid cliff scenery, picturesque villages, superb game fishing and fine sandy beaches, five of them sporting the quality Blue Flag. The **Atlantic Drive**, signposted as you leave Achill Sound, is a stunning but somewhat hair-raising road that winds along high, sheer cliffs, best undertaken on a sunny day when you can enjoy the views. It passes **Kildownet Castle** on the way to **Keel** (An Caol), the island's main resort. Between Dooega (Dumha Eige) and Keel are the **Minaun Cliffs** and the strange Cathedral Rocks; these are best explored from a sightseeing boat.

Aran Islands

Inishmore Tourist Information Office: Kilronan. Tel: 099 61263. Open: mid-Mar–early Oct, Tue–Sun 1000–1800; July–Aug, daily 1000–1900. Take a sweater or jacket on the ferry to the Aran Islands, as the return trip can be cold and wet. Sunscreen is also recommended. If you want to stay on the islands, accommodation is limited and difficult to find in high season, so book before you leave the mainland.

The three Aran Islands, formed from a limestone base similar to that of the Burren region (*see pages 150–1*), lie off the south coast of Connemara in Galway Bay. Many age-old Irish traditions are still part of everyday life here, from language and dress to methods of fishing and farming.

At 8 miles (13km) long and 2 miles (3km) wide, **Inishmore** (Inis Mór) is the largest of the three. Ferries arrive at **Kilronan** (Cill Rónáin), its main village, where passengers are met by minibuses and jaunting carts. The **Aran Heritage Centre (Ionad Arann)** (*tel: 099 61355; open: Apr–May, Sept–Oct, daily 1100–1700; June–Aug, daily 1000–1900; ££*) is a good place to learn about the history and culture of the islanders.

The island's main sight is **Dun Aengus**. This stone fort, dating from the Iron or Bronze Age, is one of Europe's most important prehistoric sites and is protected by three concentric stone battlements and sharp-pointed rock stakes designed to injure unsuspecting enemies.

Inishmaan (Inis Meáin), the middle island, with a population of around 300, also has an abundance of ancient monuments, including the fort of Dun Conor (Dun Chonchubhair). The smallest island, **Inishere** (Inis Oirr), has the ruined church of St Gobnait, the only woman allowed amongst the early Christian brethren, and the 15th-century O'Brien's Castle.

161

*Getting there: Cars cannot be taken to the Aran Islands. Passenger ferries leave daily from Rossaveel for Inishmore, with extra sailings in summer; for Inishmaan and Inishere, daily May–Sept, call **Island Ferries** (tel: 091 568903 or 561767) for winter and inter-island schedules. **Aer Arann** operates daily flights to the Aran Islands year round from Connemara Regional Airport at Inverin, near Spiddal (tel: 091 593034).*

Boyle Abbey

Main Street, Boyle. Tel: 079 63242. Open: May–Sept, Tue–Sun 1000–1700, Apr and Oct, Sat and Sun 1000–1700. ££.

Boyle's Cistercian abbey, founded in 1161, is one of Ireland's best preserved, with intact cloisters, cellars and kitchen. In Boyle itself, a charming Georgian town, there is an art gallery in King House, a beautifully restored classical mansion.

Belleek

Belleek Pottery Visitors' Centre. Tel: 028 6865 8501. Open: Mon–Fri 0900–1730 or 1800 (to 2000 in July–Aug), tours run every 20 minutes (last tour 1530 on Fri); visitor centre also open: Apr–Oct, Sat 1000–1800, Sun 1400–1800 (1100–2000 in July–Aug). ££.

Belleek is a pleasant village, the most westerly in Northern Ireland. It is famous for the **Belleek Pottery**, which produces fine Parian china and porcelain. Ireland's oldest pottery, it was established in 1857 after John Caldwell Bloomfield inherited the Castle Caldwell estate and sought to provide employment for his tenants in the aftermath of the potato famine. You can take a guided tour of the pottery to see how craftspeople design, shape and decorate the delicate basketware, vases and figurines.

Céide Fields

Tel: 096 43325. Open: mid-Mar–May and Oct, daily 1000–1700; June–Sept, daily 0930–1830; call for winter hours; last admission 45 minutes before closing. Located on the R314, 5 miles (8km) from Belderrig and 5 miles (8km) from Ballycastle; look for the silver pyramid roof rising out of the bogland. ££.

Céide (pronounced 'Cay-ja') Fields is the most extensive Stone Age monument in the world. Excavations have revealed a highly organised layout of dwellings, tombs, walls and fields covering over 3 700 acres (1 500 hectares). It represents the earliest known land enclosure, dating back some 5 500 years. Why the site was abandoned remains a mystery, but it is thought that with the growth of the bog the land could no longer support the population.

Excellent displays in the visitor centre provide background on the settlement, and a guide takes you into the fields to interpret the site. Across the road from the car park, a viewing platform affords dramatic views down over the Céide Cliffs.

Clifden

Tourist Information Office: Market Street; tel: 095 21163. Open: Apr–Sept, Mon–Sat 1000–1730; Sun 1200–1600 in July–Aug.

Set in forested hills between the mountains and the sea, on the western edge of the peninsula, Connemara's largest town is a great base for exploring the region. It's a pretty place with several good restaurants and pubs. Along the beach road are the ruins of **Clifden Castle**, built in 1815 by the town's founder, John D'Arcy, a Galway sheriff who dreamed of establishing law and order in the Connemara wilderness. The **Sky Road** is a scenic 7-mile (11-km) circular drive west of Clifden, single-track for much of the way, with spectacular views from the 'low' road above the sea or the 'high' road which climbs to over 500ft (152m).

Cong

Tourist Information Centre. Tel: 092 46542. Open: mid-Mar–Sept.

Film buffs have been making a beeline for this picturesque village in County Mayo since 1952, when it was the setting for John Ford's *The Quiet Man* starring John Wayne. The **Quiet Man Heritage Cottage** (*Circular Road; tel: 092 46089; open: Mar–Nov, daily 1000–1800; ££*) is a replica of the one used in the film. The nearby ruins of the Augustinian **Cong Abbey** date from the 13th century, and the sculpture around its doorways and window is some of the finest stone carving in Ireland. The abbey stands alongside the river and beautiful woodlands. Ashford Castle is now a luxury hotel, but its grounds are open to the public. **Corrib Cruises** sail from Cong to Inchagoill Island in Lough Corrib (*sailings at 1000, 1100, 1445 and 1700; tel: 092 46029*).

Connemara National Park

Letterfrack Visitor Centre. Tel: 095 41054. Open: Apr–May, Sept–Oct, daily 1000–1730; June 1000–1830; July–Aug 0930–1830. ££.

Covering some 4 490 acres (1 800 hectares), Connemara National Park contains expanses of bog and heath, grasslands and four peaks of the majestic Twelve Bens. The entrance to the park at Letterfrack leads to an excellent visitor centre, where there are exhibits on the nature and formation of the bogs and the park's flora and fauna. Walking trails into the glorious landscape start from the visitor centre, and there are guided walks in summer.

Connemara Heritage and History Centre

Dan O'Hara's Homestead. On the N59, 4 miles (6km) from Clifden.
Tel: 095 21246. Open: Mar–Nov, daily 1000–1800.

This visitor attraction strikes the right note between informing and entertaining. It centres around the homestead of Dan O'Hara, a Connemara farmer who was evicted for the non-payment of window tax. Forced to emigrate, his wife and three of their seven children died on the passage, and Dan ended his days selling matches on the streets of New York. After learning how the family lived in happier times, a little train takes you up the steep hill to the restored cottage.

Croagh Patrick

Croagh Patrick, rising 2 510ft (765m), is the holy mountain where St Patrick is said to have driven the snakes from Ireland (in fact, Ireland never had any snakes, as they never made it across the land bridge that briefly connected Ireland to the mainland after the last Ice Age). Every year, on Reek Sunday (the last Sunday in July), thousands of pilgrims ascend the mountain – many in bare feet – performing ritual prayers. It takes about two hours to reach the top and the views over Clew Bay and its islands are fantastic (though you can see them just as well from the statue of the saint at the start of the trail, only a 10-minute climb from the car park).

Opposite the car park in the village of Murrisk is the **National Famine Monument**, erected in 1997. John Behan's moving sculpture depicts skeletal bodies on a coffin ship, a tribute to those who died en route to America.

Galway I

Set along Galway Bay at the mouth of the River Corrib, Galway City, capital of the West, is one of the fastest growing cities in Ireland. It is also one of the most pleasant, with a compact and colourful centre that still bears traces of its medieval past. Founded in the 13th century, the city became an Anglo-Norman bastion amid the fiercely Irish lands of Connacht. Maritime trade with France and Spain brought great prosperity, especially to its 14 ruling families, known as the 'tribes of Galway'. Today, as the centre for the Gaeltacht, it's the Irish traditions that hold sway, from the hand-painted wooden shop signs along its cobbled streets to the traditional music and Irish-language theatre. It is also a lively university town and a magnet for artists and writers. The resort of Salthill, with beaches and a splendid promenade, lies just beyond the city centre.

Eyre Square

With its grassy lawns and monuments, Eyre Square is a gathering point for Galwegians. The park is known as **John F Kennedy Memorial Park**, in honour of the US president who visited here in 1963. A bronze plaque with his likeness stands at the top of the square near the **statue of Pádraic O'Conaire** (1882–1928), one of Ireland's most important literary figures, since he wrote his short stories in the Irish language. The focal point of Eyre Square is the **fountain**, erected in 1984 for the city's quincentenary. Its striking sculpture represents the rust-coloured sails of a Galway 'hooker', the region's traditional sailing boat, emphasising the importance of maritime trade to the growth of the city.

The **iron cannons** were presented to the Connaught Rangers in the 19th century for their achievements in the Crimean War. The park's entrance is through the **Browne Doorway**, which was moved here from an old mansion; it bears the arms of the Browne and Lynch families and is dated 1627.

Galway Cathedral

The Cathedral of Our Lady Assumed into Heaven and Saint Nicholas – the full name of Galway's cathedral – commands the skyline from Nun's Island, formed by channels of the River Corrib. It was one of the last cruciform churches to be built in Ireland, and was dedicated in 1965 by Boston's Cardinal Cushing. The exterior, of plain cut limestone, is a conglomeration of styles: Renaissance dome, Romanesque windows, Spanish baroque cupolas. Inside, the immense space, the massive pillars and statues and the Connemara marble flooring are all impressive.

From the Cathedral, crossing the bridge along University Road takes you to the **National University of Ireland**, built during the years of the Great Famine (1845–9). Today, it is known as a centre for Irish language and Celtic studies. The Victorian Quadrangle is its finest architectural feature.

Getting there: Tourist Information Office: Aras Failte, Victoria Place. Tel: 091 563081; fax: 091 565201. Open: May, June, Sept, 0830–1745; July–Aug, daily 0830–1945; Oct–Apr, Mon–Fri 0900–1745, Sat 0900–1245.

Galway II

Lynch Memorial

This black marble stone set above a Gothic doorway recalls the harsh justice of James Lynch Fitzstephen, Mayor of Galway in 1493, who condemned his own son to death for the murder of a Spanish sailor who had flirted with the lad's girlfriend. No one in town was willing to carry out the execution, so the mayor, determined to see the law upheld, hanged the boy himself, then became a recluse. Some say this dubious event was the origin of the term 'to lynch'.

St Nicholas' Church

The Collegiate Church of St Nicholas (*Lombard Street; open: Apr–Sept, Mon–Sat 0900–1745, Sun 1300–1745; Oct–Mar, Mon–Sat 1000–1600, Sun 1300–1600*) was built by the Normans in 1320 on the site of an older chapel. Tradition claims that Christopher Columbus prayed here before his voyage to the New World. Extensions in the 15th and 16th centuries created its unusual shape. It contains fine sculptural work and gargoyles, as well as the tomb of that sorry soul, Mayor Lynch (*see above*).

Salthill

Salthill is Galway City's seaside resort, just 2 miles (3km) west of the town centre, and a holiday destination in its own right. Many of the city's large hotels are located here. It has good beaches, nightlife and family attractions, such as **Leisureland** (*tel: 091 521455; open: daily year-round; summer 0800–2200; ££*), with a variety of pools as well as amusement park rides. Salthill's best feature is its 2$\frac{1}{2}$-mile (4-km) long promenade, the longest in Ireland. This is associated with a strange tradition: local strollers kick the wall when they reach the end of the prom. No one knows how the custom originated, but it goes back generations.

Galway by boat

Scenic cruises (daily sailings May–Sept from Woodquay; tel: 091 592447 *) aboard the* Corrib Princess *sail up the river into Lough Corrib (* see page 171 *).*

Spanish Arch

One of Galway's most famous landmarks, the Spanish Arch was built in the 16th century to protect the quays where Spanish ships unloaded their cargoes. It actually comprises two arches. At the front of the arch, adjoining the Spanish Parade, is the old fishmarket area, where Claddagh women sold the catches of the village fishermen. On the other side is the Long Walk, a promenade for the gentry in times past. Next to the arch is the new **Galway City Museum** (*tel: 091 567641; under construction at time of writing; call for opening times*).

The nearby banks of the wide, rushing river are a favourite spot for students and workers to relax on a sunny day. From the Columbus memorial, a signposted riverside walk takes you north along the River Corrib to the **Salmon Weir Bridge**. The views from the bridge are particularly wonderful from mid-April to early July, when shoals of salmon gather in the water to begin leaping their way upriver to their spawning grounds in Lough Corrib.

Knock

Tourist Information Office. Tel: 094 88193. Open: May–Sept, daily 1000–1800.

In 1879, 15 people witnessed an apparition of the Blessed Virgin in this small, impoverished town. It has since become an international **Marian Shrine**, visited by 1¹/₂ million pilgrims annually (*tel: 094 88100 for information about ceremonies and devotions; e-mail: info@knock-shrine.ie; website: www.knock-shrine.ie*). To the south of the church, the **Knock Folk Museum** (*tel: 094 88100; open: May–June, Sept–Oct, daily 1000–1800; July–Aug, daily 1000–1900; ££*) portrays life in rural Ireland in the 19th century, and documents the story of the apparition.

Kylemore Abbey

Tel: 095 41146. Open: Mar–Oct, daily 0900–1800; Nov–Feb, daily 1000–1600. ££.

Built in 1868 as a private home, Kylemore Abbey is one of Ireland's great neo-Gothic castles. In 1920 it was purchased by Benedictine nuns fleeing war-torn Belgium; they converted it into an abbey and girls' school. Two reception rooms and the main hall are open to visitors, as is the recently restored Victorian walled garden, the country's finest in its day. Also on the grounds is a Gothic church, with beautiful stained-glass windows, marble columns and intricate stone carvings. Visitors can enjoy the lake walk or watch the abbey's distinctive pottery being made in the pottery studio.

Island cruise

The **Corrib Queen** *sails from Oughterard Pier to Inchagoill Island (* **sailings at 1100, 1445 and 1700; tel: 092 552644** *). Boat trips can also be arranged with local fishermen.*

Lough Corrib

Oughterard Tourist Information Office: tel: 091 552808. Open: daily 1000–1800.

Lough Corrib is the largest lake in the Irish Republic, covering 42 000 acres (17 000 hectares). It is also among the most scenic, dotted with numerous islands. One of these, **Inchagoill**, contains early Christian monastery ruins, another a 13th-century castle. **Oughterard**, the largest town on its western shore, is a centre for brown trout and salmon fishing. The Glann road, signposted from the town centre, runs along the lakeshore for 7 miles (11km) to the **Hill of Doon**. The ruins of **Aughnanure Castle**, built around 1500, are just east of town on the shores of the lake (*tel: 091 522214; open: mid-June–mid-Sept, daily 0930–1830; ££*).

Westport

Tourist Information Centre: The Mall. Tel: 098 25711; fax: 098 26709. Open: June and Sept, Mon–Sat 0900–1800; July–Aug, Mon–Sat 0900–1700 and Sun 1000–1800; Oct–May, Mon–Fri 0900–1715.

Westport is a rare example of a planned town, designed by James Wyatt in the 18th century. The graceful tree-lined Mall which straddles the Carrowbeg river, the lovely Georgian houses and the bright shopfronts on Bridge Street make this heritage town a popular base for visitors. **Westport House and Country Estate** (*tel: 098 25430. Open: Easter–late June and late Aug–Sept, 1400–1700 or 1800; late June–late Aug, Mon–Sat 1130–1800, Sun 1400–1800; call to confirm opening days*), near the quay, is the home of Lord Sligo, a descendant of the pirate queen Grace O'Malley. The house was built in 1730 and has many outstanding features, including ceilings by Richard Castle, a dining room by James Wyatt and exquisite period furnishings. In the grounds are a children's zoo, a miniature railway and various family attractions.

Eating and drinking

Clifden

Mitchell's Restaurant

Market Street. Tel: 095 21867. Open: Mar–Oct, daily 1130–2230. ££. Seafood is superb at this popular restaurant, housed in a turn-of-the-century building with pleasant décor of wood and stone. The gigantic mound of mussels is a favourite choice, though it competes with monkfish with red pepper sauce, fresh salmon, oysters, and a variety of other fresh fish, based on the catch of the day.

Galway

McDonagh's Seafood Bar

22 Quay Street. Tel 091 565001. £–££. This Galway landmark caters for all budgets and appetites. You can relax over a restaurant meal of fresh mussels, Galway oysters or the catch of the day, or have a cheap and cheerful – but equally delicious – snack from the fish-and-chips bar.

Tigh Neachtain

17 Cross Street. Tel: 091 568820. £–££. This popular bar and bistro is housed in a historic pub in Galway's medieval quarter. The downstairs pub is famous for traditional music; the bistro upstairs serves seafood and steaks.

Westport

Kirwan's on the Mall

The Mall. Tel: 098 29077. Closed Sun. ££. Set in a converted Methodist church, this restaurant offers modern Irish cooking at its most adventurous: expect deliciously intense flavours produced from locally grown ingredients, from the humble cabbage to local smoked pork loin or fresh-caught crabs.

Torrinos

10 Market Lane, Middle Bridge Street. Tel: 098 28338. £–££. Located down a little passageway off Bridge Street, this charming Italian restaurant has a wide selection of meat, poultry and seafood dishes, pasta and gorgeous gourmet pizzas. Good wine list, and friendly attentive service. It's very popular, so book ahead in high season.

Aran sweaters

The traditional oiled wool Aran sweaters protected fishermen against the elements. Each family had their own pattern of stitches, so that the wearer could be identified in case of an accident at sea. The stitches were also symbols: for example, the cable was the fisherman's rope, for safety and good luck; the trellis stood for the stone walled fields; the diamond signified success and wealth.

Salmon and seafood

Salt Lake Manor (on the Ballyconneely road). Tel: 095 21278. Open: Apr–Sept, Mon–Sat 0900–1800; Oct–Jan, Mon–Fri 0900–1800; closed Feb/Mar. *If you are a connoisseur of smoked fish, be sure to call by and buy from this smokery renowned for its taste-packed slivers of wild salmon.*

Shopping

Galway

On Saturday mornings a lively **street market** sets up shop in the pedestrian street beside St Nicholas' Church (*0800– dusk*). The **Eyre Square Shopping Centre** has a range of offerings, from the antiques market and fashions to the heraldry gifts in the Shoemakers Tower. **Claddagh Jewellers** is one of many merchants in the area selling the traditional Claddagh rings (*see below*). The **Cornstore** in Middle Street is a complex of stylish shops; **Mulligan**, in the same street, has a good selection of traditional music.

The Claddagh ring

The Claddagh ring – two hands holding a heart with a crown on top – represents love, loyalty and friendship. This Galway tradition originated in the fishing village of Claddagh, which was located on the west bank of the river just outside the medieval walled city (now a suburb). It is said to have been made in the 1730s by Richard Joyce, who was captured by Moorish pirates and trained as a goldsmith. When King William ordered his release, he made the ring to express his gratitude. It became popular as a wedding ring and to symbolise friendship or betrothal. If the ring is worn with the heart pointing inward, it signifies the wearer's heart is taken. If the heart points outward, the wearer's heart is open.

Entertainment

Galway is a city of the arts, with several theatre groups, dance groups, a film industry and numerous arts events. One home troupe, the Druid Theatre Company, made it to Broadway with its highly acclaimed production of *The Beauty Queen of Leenane*. The **Town Hall Theatre**, Courthouse Square, is Galway's main venue for plays, concerts, films and events (*tel: 091 569777 for information and bookings*). Galway also has a vibrant music scene, where you can hear traditional Irish music or check out some excellent nightclubs with a variety of dance music.

Galway's biggest party is the **Galway Arts Festival** in July, with a variety of concerts, theatre productions, comedy, film and visual arts. Another time to catch the city in full swing is during the **Galway International Oyster Festival**, held in the latter part of September.

In **Westport** one of the most popular venues for traditional music is **Matt Molloy's**, named after and owned by a member of The Chieftains. This busy pub is on Bridge Street, and the music is in a room at the back.

A **Clifden** highlight is the **Connemara Pony Show**, held in August, with festivities celebrating this sturdy breed that evolved on the rocky slopes of the region.

Irish music and dance

Music is such an integral part of Ireland's culture that the harp is its national emblem. Traditional music can be heard throughout the country, and small towns such as Doolin and Dingle are as famed for their music pubs as cities such as Galway and Sligo. There are music festivals, called fleadhs *(pronounced 'fla') and dances, called* ceilidhs *(pronounced 'kay-lee') where you can enjoy jigs, reels, airs and laments that are centuries old, as well as revivals of the* Sean-Nós, *sung a capella in Irish, a form that nearly died out in the 1940s. Set dancing, a paired group dance, is also popular in pubs and village halls.*

Instruments

Traditional instruments include the fiddle, harp, flute, tin whistle (or penny whistle), melodeon, uillean pipes (pronounced 'ill-un'), similar to bagpipes, and the *bodhrán* (pronounced 'bow-ráwn'), a goat-skin drum shaped like a large tambourine and played with a 'tipper', or beater.

Music in Ireland is more about participation than performance. *Seisiúins* (sessions) are impromptu evenings of music and song, which usually take place in pubs. One person may begin playing a guitar, another brings out a fiddle or *bodhrán*, and soon everyone joins in. Even when the music is organised by the establishment, the audience is encouraged to participate.

International success

Bands such as The Chieftains and Clannad, and singers
such as Mary Black and Enya, have brought Irish music
to the forefront of the modern music scene, as have top
rock bands such as U2 and The Cranberries and artists
such as Van Morrison and Sinead O'Connor. Irish-American
Michael Flatley caused a sensation around the world with
his spectacular Irish dance productions, *Riverdance* and
Lord of the Dance.

The northwest

In the remote northwestern corner of Ireland, the landscape has top billing. Here the Atlantic has carved a spectacular coastline of rocky inlets and secluded beaches. There are grand peninsular drives and a heart-pounding track to the top of Europe's highest sea cliffs. When the sun breaks through, the play of light ignites blood-red cliffs and purple heathers and drapes the boglands in a cloak of tawny gold.

THE NORTHWEST

BEST OF
The northwest

Getting there: although Sligo has a railway link to Dublin, most of the northwest is virgin territory as far as the railways are concerned: buses compensate to a degree, but you'll not get far with ease without a car.

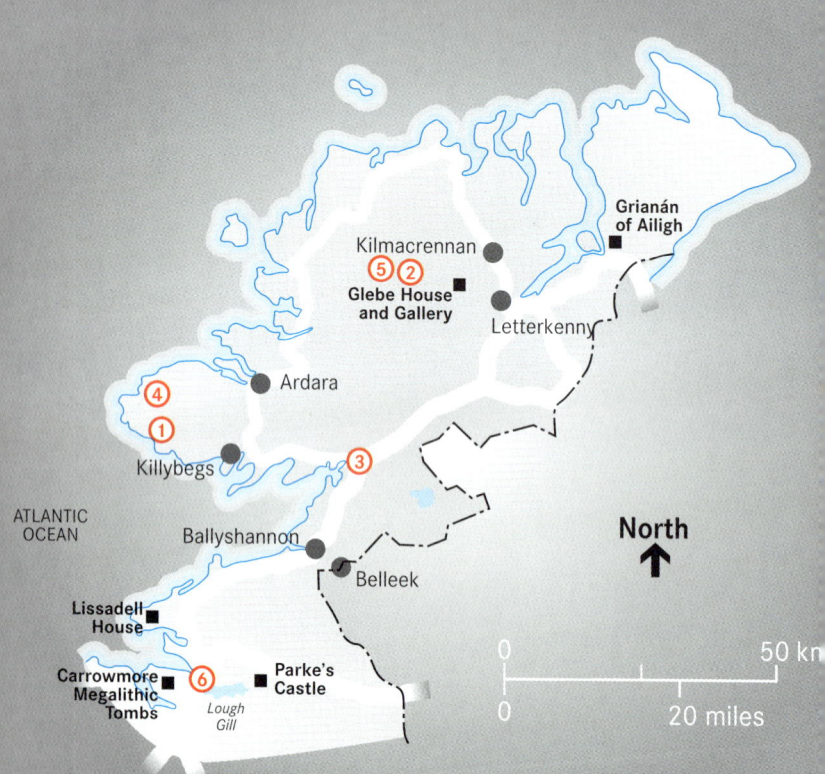

Grianán of Ailigh

Kilmacrennan

⑤ ②
Glebe House and Gallery

Letterkenny

Ardara

④

①

Killybegs

③

ATLANTIC OCEAN

Ballyshannon

Belleek

North

Lissadell House

Carrowmore Megalithic Tombs

⑥

Parke's Castle

Lough Gill

0		50 km
0	20 miles	

Bunglas cliffs

Head-spinning heights and vivid colours await at the end of the switchback road that takes you to the highest cliffs in Europe, rising to 1 972ft (601m) above the Atlantic Ocean. **Page 180**

② **Colmcille Heritage Centre**

Learn all about St Columba (known as *Colmcille* in Gaelic), the missionary who brought Christianity to Scotland, founded 37 abbeys in Ireland and kept the light of civilisation alive in the tumultuous Dark Age era. **Page 182**

③ **Donegal**

Capital of Ireland's third largest county, Donegal is little more than an overgrown village delightfully set by the water's edge. The name means 'Foreigner's Fort', though here the foreigners were the town's Viking founders, rather than the English who later controlled the town, with its abbey and castle. **Page 183**

④ **Glencolumbkille**

The 'Glen of St Colmcille's (or Columba's) Church' is a popular pilgrimage destination with a small oratory where Ireland's patron saint (one of three) lived and prayed. Even the non-religious will enjoy Glencolumbkille's folk village, illustrating rural life through 300 years. **Page 184**

 Glenveagh National Park

Glenveagh National Park has majestic mountains and not-to-be-missed gardens. In spite of the rocky landscape, there's a feeling of softness to the rounded hills and green valleys brushed by dark forests and limpid lakes. **Page 185**

⑥ **Sligo**

Sligo is synonymous with the Yeats family – W B, the poet, and the painters John (the father) and Jack (the brother). Devotees come here to trace their life and work and to take part in events run by the international summer school. **Page 189**

Ardara

Although the woollen mills and shops make Ardara (pronounced 'Ar-*drah*' by the locals) popular with visitors, its L-shaped main street retains a local rather than a touristy character and is all the more attractive for it. The village chipper (fish-and-chip shop) is the real thing, housed in a square caravan whose flattened tyres make it a permanent fixture on the main street, right across from a row of pubs with traditional music. The centre of town is known as the Diamond; this was the old market place where a monthly fair was held from 1760. Dealers came from as far away as London to purchase the region's famous tweed. The **Ardara Heritage Centre** (*on the main street; tel: 075 41262; open: daily 0930–1800; ££*) tells the story of Donegal tweed production, from sheep shearing to woven cloth, and you can watch a weaver at work. Ardara is a good base for walking holidays; the caves of Maghera and Assaranca Falls are also near by.

Bunglas cliffs

The $2^1/_2$-mile (4-km) track up to the viewpoint atop Bunglas cliffs is one of the most exciting drives in Ireland. It's not for the faint-hearted, as the narrow road runs right along the edge of these rugged cliffs, but it is well worth the terror. Bunglas is the lower side of the Slieve League cliffs which, at 1 972ft (601m), are the highest sea cliffs in Europe. There is an ample car park at the top where you can enjoy a gull's-eye view. A short path leads to an overlook down to the Giant's Desk and Chair, a rock formation in the water far below. Vertigo sufferers may want to skip the 15-minute walk to One Man's Pass, with a sheer drop on both sides. To the left of the car park, 'Tir Eire' or 'Country Ireland' is written in stone on the heather-covered banks. This was to inform aircraft in the 1940s that Ireland was a neutral country.

Carrowmore megalithic tombs

Tel: 071 61534. Open: May–Sept, daily 0930–1830. ££.

Carrowmore is Ireland's largest Stone Age cemetery. The megalithic graves here predate those at Newgrange (*see pages 64–5*) by 700 years, and are among the oldest and most important in Europe. More than 60 passage graves and dolmens have been excavated in the fields surrounding the visitor centre; many more were destroyed in the 19th century. Ring forts, standing stones and other prehistoric remains indicate that a significant hunter-gatherer settlement existed here for thousands of years. There are beautiful views of the countryside as you walk around the sites.

181

Colmcille Heritage Centre

Gartan, Churchill. Tel: 074 37306. Open: Easter and first Sun in May to last Sun in Sept, weekdays 1030–1830, Sunday 1300–1830. ££.

St Colmcille (pronounced 'colm-keel'), or Columba, is one of Ireland's three patron saints. Born a prince of Tyrconnell, he chose the life of a monk. He founded 37 monasteries in Ireland – Derry, Durrow and Kells among them – and was one of the foremost scholars of his day. It is said that his copying of a book of psalms led to a battle in which many died, and in repentance he chose the life of an exile; at the age of 42 he set sail and landed on the island of Iona off the west coast of Scotland, where he founded a monastery and brought Christianity to the Picts.

The Colmcille Heritage Centre traces the life of the saint through artistic reproductions of early monastic life and art such as manuscripts and stained glass, and looks at the rise of Christianity in Ireland. It is thought that St Colmcille was born in 521 amid the stunning landscape of Gartan Lough. A large cross marks the start of a footpath into the National Park, and there are other relics, such as the Natal Stone, near by.

Glebe House and Gallery

Churchill, Letterkenny. Tel: 074 37071. Open: Easter and mid-May–Sept, Sat–Thur 1100–1830. ££.

This Regency manor, set in woodland beside Gartan Lough, was the home of the landscape and portrait painter Derek Hill, who gave the house and its contents to the state in 1981. The house is richly furnished with William Morris wallpapers and textiles, Japanese and Islamic artworks, and unusual *objets d'art*. The gallery holds Hill's collection of 300 works by leading 20th-century artists, including ceramics and etchings by Picasso and lithographs by Kokoschka. Irish art is well represented, with paintings by Jack B Yeats and art from the Tory Islands. The 25 acres (10 hectares) of gardens are beautifully landscaped down to the lake's edge.

Donegal Town

Tourist Information Office: The Quay. Tel: 073 21148; fax: 073 22762. Open: Easter–Sept.

Donegal Town is a gateway into the wilder parts of the northwest. Its Irish name, *Dun na nGall*, means 'fort of the foreigners', a name which referred to the Vikings who set up a base here in the 9th century, but seems equally fitting today, judging by the number of visitors to this small town. It is set on a crossroads where the River Eske flows into Donegal Bay, and centred around the attractive central market square, known as the Diamond, which was built during the Plantation period in the early 17th century. The obelisk rising 20ft (6m) here is dedicated to the Four Masters. These four Franciscan friars set out to preserve as much of Celtic culture as possible and compiled one of the earliest historic texts, the *Annals of the Four Masters*, between 1632 and 1636; it is now in the National Library. The ruins of **Donegal Abbey**, the friary where they laboured, lie a few minutes' walk south of town. Beside the Diamond, **Donegal Castle** (*tel: 073 22405; open: Easter–Oct, daily 0930–1745; £*), built by an O'Donnell chieftain in the 15th century, has been restored and can be visited.

Water bus

The Harp of Erne *waterbus tour takes you on a scenic 90-minute cruise of Donegal Bay and its islands. Tickets from the booking office at Donegal Pier (* tel: 073 23666 *).*

183

Glencolumbkille

In the 1950s economic prospects in Glencolumbkille (pronounced 'glen-colm-keel') were grim but, with the help and determination of Father James McDyer, a co-operative aimed at preserving the traditional culture of the area turned a dying village into a thriving community. Its centrepiece is **An Clachan** (Father McDyer's Folk Village Museum), which is a re-created traditional village with houses of 1750, 1850 and 1900, a schoolhouse and craft shop (*tel: 073 30017; open: Easter–Sept, Mon–Sat 1000–1800, Sun 1200–1800, or by appointment; ££*). The Sheebeen sells unique homemade produce, including wines made from fuchsias and *carageen* (seaweed) and whiskey marmalade; the teahouse is renowned for its Guinness cakes. Glencolumbkille is rich in traditional music and folklore. The landscape is indeed fit for a saint, with glorious mountains and a heavenly coast that can be admired on the Seaview Drive. There is a sandy beach behind the folk museum. Walks lead into the hills where there are many archaeological sites, including some fine portal dolmens.

St Columba's Valley

According to legend, a group of demons lived in Glencolumbkille, raising a fog and turning the river into a fiery stream so that no Christian could enter. Colmcille came along and drove the demons into the sea. He founded several churches in the valley, including one on a clifftop north of the village said to have been used by the saint himself. Each year, on 9 June, St Colmcille's feast day, a turas *is performed, involving a 3-mile (5-km) walk with prayers around 15 cairns and carved stones associated with the saint.*

Glenveagh National Park

Tel: 074 37090. Open: mid-Mar–mid-Nov, daily 1000–1830. ££.

Set among the Derryveagh mountains, whose name means 'forest of oak and birch', Glenveagh National Park covers 39 500 acres (16 000 hectares) of woodland, lakes, bogs and mountains. It encompasses Donegal's highest peaks, **Mount Errigal**, rising to 2 467ft (752m) and Slieve Snacht, and is home to one of Ireland's two large red deer herds. The estate was created between 1857 and 1859 by John George Adair, who built Glenveagh Castle in 1870. The lakeside setting of this castellated mansion is magnificent, but the grounds and castle as they stand today are the work of a wealthy American businessman, Henry McIlhenny of Philadelphia, who owned the estate from 1937 to 1981.

You cannot drive within the grounds, but a shuttle bus takes you from the **visitor centre** at the entrance to the grounds, with its audio-visual show, up to the **castle**. This

remains as it was in McIlhenny's day, when he entertained film stars and aristocracy. The park's highlight is the 27 acres (11 hectares) of **gardens**, each with a different theme. There are pleasure gardens full of exotic plants, a view garden with vistas over the landscape, and the Swiss garden, a tranquil woodland path where you can hear the cuckoo and other birdsong. It's hard to tear yourself away from such beauty, so allow at least a couple of hours for the gardens, especially on a sunny day.

Grianan of Ailigh

Standing at the narrow neck of the Inishowen Peninsula, some 6 miles (10km) west of Derry, the Grianan of Ailigh is a massive circular fortress dating originally from the 5th century BC but inhabited again 1 000 years later when it became the stronghold of the O'Neill's, rulers of this strategic northernmost part of Ireland. Nineteenth-century restoration has left the fort as an impressive stone structure, with sweeping views in every direction.

Killybegs

Killybegs is the northwest's largest fishing port, and the scent of its processing industry wafts on the sea breeze, so that you will smell the town before you see it. The main street overlooks the broad harbour, which is filled with enormous fishing vessels. It's an amazing sight to watch the daily 'silver harvest' being unloaded on the pier, or simply to marvel at the array of nets, ropes and giant cables that fill the boats docked here. Needless to say, seafood is at its freshest here, so stop off at one of the pubs or chippers set around the pleasant town centre.

Letterkenny

Tourist Information Office: Derry Road. Tel: 074 21160; fax: 074 25180. Open: all year.

With its long main street, Letterkenny is the largest town in Donegal and one of the fastest growing in all of Ireland. The neo-Gothic cathedral of St Eunan dominates the town, with its soaring spire and mix of French-style architecture and Celtic-inspired stone carvings. The small **County Museum** (*High Road; tel: 074 24613; open: Mon–Sat 1030–1615; £*) has a good archaeology collection.

Lissadell House

Tel: 071 63150. Open: June–mid-Sept, Mon–Sat 1030–1215, 1400–1615. ££.

An atmosphere of faded grandeur exists behind the imposing façade of 'that old Georgian mansion', as described by W B Yeats. It is still owned by the Gore-Booth family, and houses many artefacts spanning several generations. Yeats was a frequent visitor here, calling on the two sisters, Eva and Constance, immortalised in one of his poems. Constance was a revolutionary who participated in the Easter Rising and became the first woman elected to the British House of Commons. Murals of the sisters and other members of the family were painted on the dining-room wall by Constance's husband, Count Casimir Markievicz. The house is surrounded by beautiful woodlands stretching down to the lake.

187

Parke's Castle

Tel: 071 64149. Open: Apr–Sept, daily 0930–1630; Oct, 1000–1700. ££.

The finest thing about Parke's Castle is its setting, right at the water's edge of Lough Gill. Built in 1609, this fortified manor house set within a walled enclosure is typical of Irish plantation settlements. It was erected on the site of an earlier O'Rourke stronghold, whose clan chief was executed for having extended his hospitality to a shipwrecked officer of the Spanish Armada. His confiscated lands were then granted to Captain Robert Parke. The castle has been restored using Irish oak and traditional craftsmanship. The stone-mullioned windows, diamond-shaped chimneys and parapet walls are some of its outstanding features. The interior contains an exhibition on the castle's restoration and the topography and archaeology of the surrounding countryside.

Lough Gill cruise

Wild Rose Waterbus Tours operates from Parke's Castle, offering cruises around Lough Gill and the Isle of Innisfree (daily sailings in season, 1230–1830).

Sligo Town

Tourist Information Office: Temple and Charles Streets. Tel: 071 61201; fax: 071 60360. Open: Mon–Fri 0900–1300, 1400–1700.

The northwest's largest town spans the River Garavogue and covers the neck of land between Lough Gill and Sligo Bay. It's a lively place, with a booming economy, a college and a compact town centre of traditional façades. The town is also known as a centre for the arts and for Irish music. Its greatest appeal for many visitors is its associations with W B Yeats. At Hyde Bridge a striking bronze statue of the poet by Rohan Gillespie stands across from the **Yeats Memorial Building**, where the Yeats Summer School of poetry readings, lectures and other events is held in August.

The **Sligo Art Gallery** (*Yeats Memorial Building, Hyde Bridge; tel: 071 45847; open: Mon–Sat 1000–1700; £*) holds contemporary art exhibitions. The **Yeats Gallery Library Building** (*Stephen Street; tel: 071 42212; open: Tue–Fri 1000–1700, Sat 1000–1300, 1400–1700*) is home to a large collection of paintings by Jack B Yeats, the poet's brother, and their father John B Yeats. Personal memorabilia are displayed in the museum. **Sligo Abbey** (*tel: 071 46406; open: June–Sept, daily 0930–1830; ££*) founded in 1253, is the only medieval building remaining in the town, and most of the ruins date from the 15th century. The cloisters and altar have beautifully carved stonework. Other notable buildings include the court-house, Dominican friary and several churches.

The brothers Yeats

The poet William Butler Yeats (1865–1939) and his artist brother, Jack (1871–1957), were members of a prominent Sligo family. Although they spent their childhood in London, where their father John struggled to earn a living as a portrait painter, during summer holidays they visited their maternal grandparents, the Pollexfens, who were merchant shippers in Sligo. This idyllic landscape inspired them throughout their lives. Jack, one of Ireland's foremost 20th-century painters, declared 'Sligo was my school, and the sky above it'. W B credited Sligo as the inspiration for the poems that earned him the Nobel Prize for Literature in 1923.

Eating and drinking

Donegal

McGroarty's Bar

The Diamond. Tel: 073 21049. Lunch, May–Sept, 1200–1700, Oct–Apr, 1200–1500. Snacks served all day. £. This traditional bar, housed in a stone building on the main square, known as the Diamond, caters for vegetarians, a rare thing in Ireland. Along with smoked salmon and a variety of sandwiches and casseroles, there is a long list of creative vegetarian dishes to choose from, all fresh and prepared to order, including salads, quiches, stir-fry, pitta bread wraps and soups.

Killybegs

The Fleet Inn

Tel: 073 31518. ££. This restaurant above the pub of the same name works miracles with the fish that comes off the local boats, whether your tastes are for something traditional – mackerel with champ (that's potatoes mashed with onions) – or the succulent novelty of scallops with ginger cream.

Melly's

On the main street, across from the car park. Tel: 073 31093. Open: to 2230. £. For fish so fresh it melts in your mouth, try this bright and cheerful chipper which looks out over the harbour. Melly's also serves quiche, chicken, desserts and weekday café lunches.

Letterkenny

Mount Errigal Hotel

Ballyraine, Letterkenny. Tel: 074 22700; fax: 074 25085. ££. Good bar meals are to be had here, or you can try the seafood and other popular Irish dishes served in the pleasant Glengesh Restaurant, with its à la carte or set three-course menu. Facilities also include a leisure centre with a 72-ft (22-m pool) and a nightclub.

Pat's on the Square

9 Market Square. Tel: 074 21761. Closed Mon in winter. ££. Pat's specialises in pizza, though it also offers pasta dishes. Some of the gourmet pizzas work a treat: 'Black and Blue' (Cashel Blue cheese and walnut topping) is a delicious nutty cream blend. 'Ireland's Own', combining ham, cheese, herbs and roast potato, is the hungry traveller's friend.

Sligo

Sligo is a great place to eat, with lots of good food shops (entering **Cosgroves**, at 32 Market Square, is like stepping back in time several decades), plus a Friday market, and several eating places that will not cost an arm and a leg. For lunchtime treats – garlic mushrooms, smoked chicken, all sorts of filled baguettes — try the **Yeats River Café** (*The Mall; closed Sun; £*). For modern Mediterranean food, plus pizzas, pasta and the like, try the **Garavogue** (*Stephen Street; tel: 071 40100; ££*).

Shopping

Donegal

Magee of Donegal, established in 1866, is famous for its hand-woven tweed jackets, which are reasonably priced at its shop on the Diamond. Outside town, on the Ballyshannon Road, **Donegal Craft Village** is a group of workshops making batik, pottery, jewellery and uillean pipes among other goods.

Entertainment

Nancy's pub in **Ardara** is legendary for its music and its food (*Front Street; tel: 075 41187*).

Sport in Ireland

'Rugby is a game for ruffians played by gentlemen
Soccer is a game for gentlemen played by ruffians
Gaelic football is a game for ruffians played by ruffians
But hurling is a game for gentlemen played by gentlemen.'

So goes an old saw about Ireland's national sport. **Hurling** is similar to hockey and is played on turf. Each team has 15 players who use a flat stick with a wide base, called a hurley, or *camán*, to carry or handle a hard leather ball, called a *sliothár*; the aim is to score points by getting the ball inside the goal or over the crossbar. Because it demands great strength and skill, it is one of the most exciting field sports.

Gaelic football, a cross between football and rugby, is another highly popular team sport. The Gaelic Athletic Association (GAA) was founded in 1884 to boost the national identity through these sports, which had been played in Ireland's towns and parishes down the centuries. Ireland also lays claim to inventing the game of **rugby**, first played in universities and public schools in the 1860s.

Horses and dogs

The first steeplechase was run in Ireland in 1752, so called because it took place between two church steeples. Since then **horse racing** has become Ireland's favourite spectator sport. There are 25 racecourses in Ireland, and there is hardly a day in the year when a race isn't held somewhere around the country. The two most famous meetings are the Irish Classics at the Curragh in County Kildare, and the Irish Grand National at Fairyhouse in County Meath. Information on various courses and meetings is available from the tourist offices.

Greyhound racing is also popular, with 18 tracks around the country (*for further information, contact Bord na gCon, Irish Greyhound Racing Board, 104 Henry Street, Limerick; tel: 061 316788; fax: 061 316739*).

Golf

When it comes to golf courses, Ireland has some beauties. There are some 360 courses of varying sizes and difficulties around the country, many of them challenging links courses set alongside the sea, making Ireland second only to Scotland in the amount of **golf greens** per square mile. Top courses include Portmarnock near Dublin, Ballybunion in County Kerry and Royal County Down and Royal Portrush in Northern Ireland. The tourist information offices provide details of golf facilities in their areas.

Walking and beaches

Ireland is a walker's paradise, with unspoiled forests, hills, mountains and open countryside. Information on **walks** for all levels of ability is available from the tourist offices (or from *Walking/Cycling Ireland, PO Box 5520, Ballsbridge, Dublin 4; tel: 01 668 8278; fax: 01 660 5566*). Ireland's coastline is dotted with many **Blue Flag beaches**, the European symbol of quality, and watersports are also popular on several inland lakes. Other popular activities include cycling, angling, sailing and horse riding. Many stables offer riding lessons for all levels of ability.

Useful addresses

For information on angling, contact the Irish Tourist Board in the UK (PO Box 19, Rugby CV23 0P2 *). Boating enthusiasts can get further information from The Irish Sailing Association (* 3 Park Road, Dun Laoghaire, Co Dublin; tel: 01 280 0239; fax: 01 280 7558 *).*

193

Northern Ireland

For so long overshadowed by politics, Northern Ireland is only now beginning to return to its rightful place as a wonderful land to visit. This is a compact region of great contrasts, with mountains, lakes, waterfalls and dramatic cliffs aplenty, plus fabulous country houses and gardens, museums and nature reserves, and the bright lights of buzzing Belfast.

BEST OF
Northern Ireland

Getting there: **Belfast International Airport** *at Aldergrove is 19 miles (30km) from the city centre, a 30-minute drive on the M2. There is a shuttle service between the airport and city centre (tel: 028 9442 2888).* **Belfast City Airport** *is 3 miles (5km) from the city centre and can be reached by train from Great Victoria Street station (tel: 028 9045 7745). There is a regular rail service between Belfast and Dublin and other cities in Northern Ireland and the Republic: Northern Ireland Railways (enquiries tel: 028 9089 9411).*

① Belfast

Once known as the 'Big Smoke' because of its shipyards and linen factories, modern Belfast combines the best of the past – exuberant Victorian pubs, theatres and opera houses – with all that is vibrant and modern as the newly confident city relishes peace after decades of 'The Troubles'.
Pages 198–203

② Bushmills

Even if whiskey is not your tipple, there is a great deal of enjoyment to be had from a visit to what claims to be 'the world's oldest distillery'. Ireland's history is bound up with the story of the 'water of life', introduced by monks and enjoyed in many a home and pub.
Page 204

③ Derry

The Corporation of London built the historic city of Derry, which has the finest medieval walls in Ireland – indeed, in all of Europe, standing to a height of 26ft (8m) and encircling the attractive old walled city.
Pages 206–7

④ Downpatrick

Sacred to all the Irish, Downpatrick is the burial place of no less than three of the medieval world's most influential saints – Patrick, Brigid and Columba, the founders of Celtic monasteries and convents that kept the flame of classical learning alive during the Dark Ages.
Page 209

⑤ Enniskillen

Set between Lower and Upper Lough Erne, Enniskillen is picture-book Ireland, a town where water and green hills meet to compose a picture of rural serenity, best enjoyed from the park and hills to the east of the town. **Page 210**

⑥ Giant's Causeway

Ireland's most famous and most visited site is a place of inspiring beauty, born of the fire of the volcanoes that formed the earth, then eroded into nature's own work of art by ice and storms.
Pages 212–13

⑦ Mount Stewart

The gardens at Mount Stewart are among Europe's finest, full of rare plants that thrive in the gentle Gulf Stream climate of Ireland's east coast, planted to make the most of the marvellous views over Strangford Lough. **Page 217**

⑧ Newcastle and the Mountains of Mourne

Heather-clad moorland interspersed with rolling green hills, and sheltered fishing villages set alongside sweeping sands make the area around Newcastle and the Mountains of Mourne a paradise for those who love the combination of mountain and coastal scenery.
Page 217

⑨ Ulster American Folk Park

Celebrating Ireland's long connections with America, this open-air museum contrasts the life of emigrants and their families on both sides of the Atlantic through reconstructed ships, houses, streetscapes and churches, with costumed guides to bring the story to life. **Page 220**

Tourist information
Northern Ireland Tourist Board, *St Anne's Court, 59 North Street. Tel: 028 9024 6609; fax: 028 9031 2424.*

Belfast I

Overshadowed by the political affairs of Northern Ireland, Belfast is often avoided as a holiday destination.

This is a pity, for what emerges from the smokescreen of the past Troubles is a vibrant city with much to offer. Belfast enjoys a lovely setting on the shores of a sea lough, backed by green hills. It is young as Irish cities go, dating largely from the 19th century when it flourished as a port and commercial centre, the linen mills and shipyards forming the backbone of its wealth. Belfast today has a fine university, a top arts festival and a lively nightlife, with smart, sophisticated bars and restaurants standing alongside the characterful Victorian saloons.

City Hall

Donegall Square. Tel: 028 9027 0465. Guided tours June–Sept, Mon–Fri 1030, 1130, 1430 and Sat 1430; Oct–May, Mon–Sat 1430. Tours last approximately one hour. £.

This grand Renaissance-style building, with its façade of Portland stone, was built in 1906. Even if you're not taking in one of the free guided tours, step inside for a look at the stained-glass windows, decorative plasterwork and ornate **central dome**, rising 173ft (53m) high from the foyer. To the right of the entrance is a small exhibition about the city. You can pick up a guide to the statues and monuments that adorn the spacious grounds. These include the **Titanic Memorial** on the building's east side.

Public transport

Citybus provides a regular service to all parts of the Belfast area. Tickets can be bought from the driver, or multi-journey tickets are available in local shops or at the Citybus kiosk in Donegall Square West (enquiries tel: 028 9024 6485). Taxis look like London black cabs and have a yellow disc on the windscreen. If your taxi does not have a meter, be sure to ask the fare before setting off.

Botanic Gardens

Tel: 028 9032 4902. Gardens open: dawn–dusk; Palm House and Tropical Ravine open: Apr–Sept, weekdays 1000–1700, weekends 1300–1700; closed for lunch 1200–1300; closed at 1600 in winter. £.

Belfast's Botanic Gardens were laid out in 1827 between Queen's University and the River Lagan. Here, paths lined with wrought-iron benches wind past shady trees, flower beds and a rose garden. The **Palm House**, designed by Charles Lanyon in 1839, is one of the earliest curvilinear glass and cast-iron glasshouses. A variety of temperate species billows into the 49-ft (15-m) high dome, added in 1852. By contrast, you'll gaze down into the **Tropical Ravine** from a steamy walkway lush with hanging vines and exotic flowers.

Getting there: Tourism Development Office: Belfast City Council, The Cecil Ward Building, Linenhall Street. Tel: 028 9032 0202; fax: 028 9027 0325.

Belfast II

Crown Liquor Saloon

*Great Victoria Street. Bar meals served Mon–Sat 1200–1500. Flannigan's
Eatery and Bar (above the saloon), full menu Mon–Sat 1200–2100, Sun
1230–1900. £.*

You'll be ready for a pint after a look at this dazzling Victorian
bar, opposite the Opera House. Now owned by the National
Trust, it is the most perfectly preserved bar of its era in
the province. A visit here is like entering a kaleidoscope of
bright stained glass, gleaming brasswork, geometric Italian
tilework, embossed ceilings and bevelled mirrors.

Grand Opera House

*Great Victoria Street. Tel: 028 9024 9129 (programme information);
028 9024 1919 (tickets).*

It's worth seeing a show just for the privilege of sitting in
this opulent opera house, designed in 1894 by Frank
Matcham. Lavish gilt mouldings, ornamental plasterwork,
and a magnificent frescoed ceiling by Irish artist Cherith
McKinstry are all part of its Victorian glory. The elephants
supporting the boxes and the imitation Sanskrit add an
oriental touch.

Linenhall Library

17 Donegall Square. Tel: 028 9032 1707. Open: Mon–Fri 0930–1800 ('til 2030 on Thur), Sat 0930–1600. £.

Housed in a charming building on Donegall Square, Belfast's oldest library has been lending books since 1788. It houses local history and literature collections as well as an extensive archive of documents relating to the Troubles. A visit here is a must for anyone who cherishes the atmosphere of old-fashioned reading rooms, which are rapidly becoming an endangered species around the world. The library is for members' use only, but you can go in for a look around, a browse through the day's newspapers and a cup of coffee in the little café.

Parks

Despite – or perhaps because of – its industrial origins, Belfast has a wealth of parks in or near the city centre. In addition to the Botanic Gardens, there is **Sir Thomas and Lady Dixon Park**, fragrant with over 20 000 roses; **Ormeau Park**, the city's oldest and one of its largest parks; **Grovelands Park**, with heather and alpine gardens; **Lagan Meadows**, a wildlife haven with woodland, marsh and meadows; and **Barnett Demesne**, a landscaped estate. To the north of the city, Belfast Castle is set within **Cave Hill Country Park**, with nature reserves and archaeological sites among the heath, moors and woodland.

Queen's University

Visitor Centre, Botanic Avenue. Tel: 028 9033 5252. Open: May–Sept, Mon–Sat 1000–1600; Oct–Apr, weekdays only. £.

Botanic Avenue is one of Belfast's nicest streets, lined with attractive restaurants, bars and shops that cater for a university clientele. The street leads into Queen's University, with its handsome Tudor-revival buildings designed by Charles Lanyon and built in 1849. Its highlights are the red-brick and sandstone main building, and University Square, an impressive terrace. There are exhibitions in the Visitor Centre.

Belfast III

St Anne's Cathedral

Donegall Street. Tel: 028 9032 8332. Open: 0800–1700. £.

The construction of this Neo-Romanesque cathedral, begun in 1899, was directed by 8 architects over 80 years, and is still not entirely finished. Basilican in plan, its sombre character is somewhat relieved by an ornately carved west front, a decorative baptistery and some fine stained glass and 1920s mosaics.

Ulster Museum

Stranmillis Road, Botanic Gardens. Tel: 028 9038 3000. Open: Mon–Fri 1000–1700, Sat 1300–1700, Sun 1400–1700. £.

This major national museum, located in a corner of the Botanic Gardens, has three floors devoted to the history and natural history of Northern Ireland, and a fine art collection on the top floor. A highlight is the treasure horde from the wrecked Spanish Armada ship, the *Girona*. The ground floor is taken up by the massive machinery and equipment that powered Belfast's industrial age and the linen industry. A skeleton of an Irish giant deer, a long-extinct species, is the most remarkable exhibit in the natural history section.

Also worth exploring

Belfast Zoo is a fun day out for the children. The Giant's Ring is a neolithic circular earthwork with a dolmen in the centre, just 4 miles (6km) outside the city centre. Stormont, Northern Ireland's Parliament House, can only be visited by advance arrangement, but you can view its impressive façade of Portland stone from the Newtownards Road (A20).

Walk

The grounds of the magnificent **City Hall** (*see page 198*) fill **Donegall Square** and make a pleasant place to sit. Surrounding the square are some of Belfast's grandest buildings. At No 1, on the north side, **Marks & Spencer** occupies one of the great linen warehouses of the 19th century. The **Linenhall Library** (*see page 201*) is at No 17. On the west side is the baroque **Scottish Provident Institution**, built in 1899; to the east is the Gothic **Pearl Assurance** building of the same date, and on the south side **Jaffe Brothers** is housed in another linen warehouse decorated with busts of Isaac Newton and Christopher Columbus, among others.

Walk north along Donegall Place, a pedestrianised shopping street, and turn right on Castle Place. As you reach Cornmarket you may hear a band playing in the afternoon. Carry straight on into **High Street**, and explore the little 'entries' or narrow lanes running through to Ann Street. Here you'll find small shops and some of Belfast's most characterful pubs, such as White's Tavern, the city's oldest pub, along Winecellar Entry.

At the end of High Street is the **Albert Memorial Clock Tower**, called 'the Albert Clock' by locals, a tribute to Queen Victoria's consort. This well-loved landmark leans slightly, due to its foundation on wooden piles driven into the muddy reclaimed land. Behind it is the **Custom House**, designed by Sir Charles Lanyon in 1854. You can also see Samson and Goliath, two enormous yellow cranes in Harland & Wolff's shipyards on Queen's Island. The ill-fated ocean liner *Titanic* was built there.

Armagh

Armagh is a name most recently associated with religious conflict, but this beautiful city holds an important place in history as the site of a church founded by St Patrick in AD 455. Of the two cathedrals now located here, the neo-Gothic Catholic church is the one that dominates the view with its twin spires, but the Protestant one is the older, being the last resting place of the warrior Brian Boru, King of Ireland and famous for defeating the Vikings in 1014.

Some 4km (2.5 miles) west of Armagh is another very early site: **Navan Fort** dates from the Bronze Age and was an important ritual site in the Iron Age, later associated with the mythical hero, Cuchulainn. Learn all about the site at the excellent visitor centre (*tel: 028 3752 5550*).

Bushmills

Bushmills the town grew up around Bushmills, the distillery. The former is an attractive small town set on the River Bush, which teems with salmon and trout. The latter is the world's oldest legal whiskey distillery, granted a licence by King James I in 1608, but the famous *aqua vitae* is known to have been made here as early as the 13th century. You can take a guided tour of the **Old Bushmills Distillery** (*tel: 012657 31521; open: Apr–Oct, Mon–Sat 0930–1730, Sun 1200–1730, last tour 1600 each day; Nov–Mar, Mon–Fri, 5 tours daily at 1030, 1130, 1330, 1430, 1530; ££*) to see how this leading malt whiskey is made, and learn about the processes of mashing, fermentation, distillation, maturation and bottling. There's a whiskey tasting at the end.

The water of life

Uisce Beatha, which means the 'water of life' in Gaelic, has been produced for over a thousand years. The raw materials for making it are barley and pure water, and it is these two ingredients that give individual products their unique character. For example, the water from St Columb's Rill, a tributary of the River Bush, is said to give Bushmills its special flavour. Apart from the 'e' in the spelling, Irish Malt Whiskey differs from its Scottish counterpart in two main ways. The barley is dried in closed kilns without the use of a peat fire, so the characteristic smoky taste of many Scotch whiskies is absent. Irish whiskies are generally distilled three times, as opposed to twice for most Scottish brands.

Carrickfergus

Situated on Belfast Lough, south of Larne, Carrickfergus has an attractive harbour and several visitor attractions, of which the most dominant is the waterside castle. Children will love the Knight Ride experience in Antrim Street (*tel: 028 9335 1273*) which takes visitors on a cable-car ride through the town's often-bloody history.

205

Castle Coole

2 miles (3km) from Enniskillen on the A4. Tel: 01365 322690. Open: May–Aug, Fri–Wed 1300–1800, last tour 1715; also open: Easter and Sept weekends. ££.

Set in a landscaped park amidst oak woodlands southeast of Enniskillen, this splendid neo-classical mansion is considered to be one of Ireland's finest houses. It was designed in the 1790s for the 1st Earl of Belmore, and is largely the work of the English architect James Wyatt. Portland stone for the grand façade was shipped from Dorset to Donegal and transported overland. The colonnaded pavilions that frame the central block and portico create a graceful symmetry. Its glory, however, is the lavish interior, adorned with richly ornamented plasterwork and containing nearly all of the original furniture and portraiture.

Derry

Tourist Information Office: 44 Foyle Street. Tel: 028 7126 7284, fax: 028 7137 7992. Open: Easter–June, Mon–Thur 0900–1715, Fri 0900–1700, Sat 1000–1700; July–Sept, Mon–Fri 0900–1900, Sat 1000–1800, Sun 1000–1700; Oct–Easter, Mon–Thur 0900–1715, Fri 0900–1700. The centre offers walking tours (££) of the historic city lasting 1 1/2 hours, June–Oct, Mon–Fri 1030 and 1430.

The highlights of this historic city are best seen on a walk around the top of the **town walls**, a circuit of about a mile (1.5km). Completed in 1618, they stand 20ft (6m) high and were never breached, despite three sieges, one of which – the 105-day Siege of Derry, which began in December 1688 – was the longest in British history. Panels set into the wall near the eight bastions and four original gates explain the historical background of the nearby buildings and features such as the great cannon, *Roaring Meg*. From the ramparts there are sweeping views across the great swathe of housing estates that comprises much of modern-day Derry.

The centre of the walled city is **The Diamond**, with a memorial to those who died in the two World Wars. The **Tower Museum** (*Union Hall Place; tel: 028 7137 2411; open: Sept–June, Tue–Sat 1000–1700; July–Aug, Mon–Sat*

1000–1700; ££), housed in the 17th-century O'Doherty's Tower, tells the 'Story of Derry' from ancient to modern times. The **Fifth Province** (*Calgach Centre, Butcher Street; tel: 028 7137 3177; open: 1000–1630; ££*), is a high-tech exhibition that brings Celtic history and culture to life. The **Harbour Museum** (*Guildhall Street and Harbour Square; tel: 028 7137 7331; open: Mon–Fri 1000–1300, 1400–1630; £*) focuses on the region's maritime history.

St Columb's Cathedral (*Bishop Street; tel: 028 7126 7313; open: Mar–Oct 0900–1700; Nov–Feb 0900–1600; closed 1300–1400*), built in 1633, is one of the earliest Protestant cathedrals and contains the country's oldest and largest bells. It has many relics from the Siege of Derry, including an enormous mortar ball fired over the wall, and other treasures in the Chapter House Museum.

207

Devenish Island

Devenish Island ferry: Trory Point, 2 miles (3km) north of Enniskillen. Tel: 028 6634 3700. Open: Apr–Sept, Tue–Sun. ££. Pull up at the pier and the ferry will come to meet you.

The monastery founded on this tiny island by St Molaise in the 6th century was one of the most important in Ulster and, despite Viking attacks, it remained so into the early 17th century. Its finest structure is the 12th-century round tower, with five storeys rising 82ft (25m) high. Look for the human faces carved above the four windows at the top, a unique feature. Other surviving buildings include the Teampall Mor church near the jetty and 15th-century St Mary's Priory, with a carved stone cross near by.

St Patrick

St Patrick was a Roman Briton, born into a wealthy Christian family near Hadrian's Wall in the early 5th century. As a youth he was captured by Irish raiders and spent six years as a slave. He escaped, became a priest, and at the age of about 30 returned to Ireland as a bishop around the year 432. After founding his first church at Saul in County Down, he travelled throughout Ireland, converting the Celtic chieftains to Christianity. Although the details of Patrick's life are uncertain, he is known to have preached in Ireland for 30 or 40 years and died before the end of the century.

Downpatrick

Tourist Information Office: Market Street. Tel: 028 4461 2233. Open: all year.

The modern town sprawls below the Hill of Down, which is topped by **Down Cathedral** (*English Street; tel: 028 4461 4922; open: Mon–Sat 0900–1700, Sun 1400–1700; £*), founded as a Benedictine monastery in the 12th century, and rebuilt in the 18th and 19th centuries in the Gothic style. Among its features are a medieval baptismal font, a unique pulpit on which the Telford organ is built, return chapter stalls and Georgian box pews. The **churchyard** is the reputed burial place of Ireland's three patron saints: Patrick, Brigid and Columcille (Columba). An enormous stone (placed here in 1900) with the inscription 'Patric' marks the site where the Norman knight John de Courcy re-interred their bones in the 12th century, fulfilling a prophecy that the three would be buried in the same place.

On the road below the cathedral is the **Down County Museum** (*The Mall, English Street. Tel: 028 4461 5218; open: Sept–May, Tue–Fri 1100–1700, Sat 1400–1700; June–Aug, Mon–Fri 1100–1700, Sat–Sun 1400–1700; ££*). It is housed in the old county gaol, which was built between 1789 and 1796 and is the most complete example of its era in Ireland. A tableau of prison life has been re-created in the Cell Block. In the gatehouse, the **St Patrick Heritage Centre** traces the life of the saint. The alleged site of his first church is 2 miles (3km) away at the village of **Saul**. Other sites in the area include **Struell Wells**, a pagan holy well blessed by Patrick; the hill of **Slieve Patrick**, a pilgrimage site with a statue of the saint at the summit, and the ruins of **Inch Abbey**, in a pretty marshland setting.

Enniskillen

Fermanagh Tourist Information Centre: Wellington Road. Tel: 028 6632 3110; fax: 028 6632 5511.

Fermanagh's capital is an attractive town built on an island between Upper and Lower Lough Erne. Traditional pubs and red-brick Georgian buildings line Townhall and High Streets, its main thoroughfares. **Enniskillen Castle** (*tel: 028 6632 5000; open: May, June and Sept, Mon–Sat 1400–1700, Tue–Fri 1000–1700; July–Aug, Mon and weekends 1400–1700, Tue–Fri 1000–1700; Oct–Apr, Mon 1400–1700, Tue–Fri 1000–1700; ££*), built by the Maguire chieftains in the 16th century, has a striking watergate with corbelled towers and turrets. It houses a heritage centre, county museum and the Royal Inniskilling Fusiliers Museum. In the old **Buttermarket** (*tel: 028 6632 383; open: Mon–Sat 0930–1730*), you can watch craftspeople at work in the Enniskillen Craft and Design Centre. Oscar Wilde and Samuel Beckett attended the **Portora Royal School**, established in 1608; it lies across the West Bridge. Atop a hill on the east side of town, the **Cole Monument**, a tall Doric column, has fine views over the town.

Florence Court

Tel: 028 6634 8249. House open: May–Aug, Wed–Mon 1300–1800; grounds open, all year. ££.

This neo-classical mansion was built in the mid-18th century by John Cole and named after his English wife. Their son, who became the 1st Earl of Enniskillen, added the arcades and pavilions flanking the central house in the 1770s. The state rooms were decorated with flamboyant rococo plasterwork by John West, painstakingly restored after a fire in 1955. The house is surrounded by hills and beautiful grounds; there are several walks and nature trails, one of which leads to the Florence Court yew tree, progenitor of all Irish yews.

Glenariff Forest Park

Tel: 028 2175 8232. Open: daily until 2000. ££ for parking.

Glenariff, the 'queen of the glens', is arguably the most beautiful of the nine Antrim glens. It covers 2 928 acres (1 185 hectares), more than three-quarters of which have been planted with trees. The main species is Sitka spruce, a North American conifer, which flourishes on the poor soil, but areas of old broad-leaved woodland also exist in the park. There are small lakes and recreation areas, rocky gorges and spectacular waterfalls created by two rivers, the Inver and the Glenariff. The glen has been designated a national nature reserve. Trails from half a mile to 5 miles long (1–9km) start from the car park. There is also a visitor centre.

Giant's Causeway

This incredible geological phenomenon is the most visited sight in Northern Ireland. It is said that the Giant's Causeway was built by the legendary giant Finn McCool in order to lure his rival Benandonner to Ireland for a battle. When the Scottish giant arrived, he was bigger than expected, so Finn's wife Oonagh swaddled her frightened husband in a blanket, covered his head with a large bonnet and rocked him in an enormous cradle. Benandonner was so terrified by the size of this 'baby' that he had no desire to meet its father. He fled back to Scotland, ripping up the causeway as he went to avoid pursuit.

NORTHERN IRELAND

In reality, the 40 000 basalt columns that make up the Giant's Causeway were formed by the cooling and cracking of lava from a volcanic explosion some 60 million years ago. They form a series of stepping stones reaching far into the sea, following the underwater fissure and resurfacing at the Scottish island of Staffa.

When you see the causeway for the first time, you may be surprised to find that it is not as big as you were led to expect from all those well-composed guidebook photographs. What is most impressive are the shapes of this army of columns and its dramatic backdrop of cliffs, which rise as high as 328ft (100m).

There are two approaches. It's an easy half-mile (1-km) walk on the road leading down from the visitor centre (take the shuttle bus if you prefer). Alternatively, a longer path takes you along the top of the cliffs and down the Shepherd's Steps – all 162 of them – where you'll have splendid views of the cliff-face columns known as the Organ. It's worth walking the extra 547yds (500m) to the Port Reostan viewpoint for a spectacular vista back across the causeway. Near here, at Port na Spaniagh, is the wreck of the Spanish Armada galleon, the *Girona*, whose treasure horde can be seen in the Ulster Museum in Belfast (*see page 202*). The visitor centre has interpretative displays and an audio-visual theatre.

Getting there: Tourist Information Office. Tel: 028 2073 1855. Open: all year. Visitor Centre, tel: 028 2073 1582. Site accessible all year; Visitor Centre open: Mar–May and Sept–Oct, daily 1000–1700; June 1000–1800; July–Aug 1000–1900. ££ for parking.

Walking

A spectacular 10-mile (16-km) walk along the Causeway Coast runs from the Giant's Causeway to White Park Bay, passing dramatic cliffs and coastal scenery and the ruins of Dunseverick Castle.

Lisburn

Tourist Information Office: Market Square. Tel: 028 9266 0038. Open: all year.

Lisburn is an attractive town with fine parks whose main attraction is the **Irish Linen Centre and Lisburn Museum** (*Market Square; tel: 028 9266 3377; open: Mon–Sat, 0930–1700; £*), where the 'Flax to Fabric' exhibition tells the story of the region's great linen industry, which flourished for over 200 years until the costly production process eventually led to a decline in demand. Today, only small quantities are produced for the luxury goods market. You can watch the weavers plying this ancient trade in the hand-loom workshop. The museum also covers the history and culture of the region. Behind the centre is **Christ Church Cathedral**. Built in 1623, it is a good example of the so-called Planters' Gothic style; the spire was added in the early 19th century. There are many Huguenot graves in the churchyard.

Lough Erne

Lower Lough Erne, sprinkled with nearly a hundred tiny islands, forms a broad arc from Belleek (*see page 162*) to the county town of Enniskillen, where it is joined to Upper Lough Erne by a narrow channel. It provides an important habitat for wildlife and a fine playground for visitors. The fishing is superb, and several country parks and forests dotted around the shore offer peaceful woodland walks, hidden castle ruins and outdoor activities. Boatmen ferry visitors out to the islands to see early Christian monastic ruins, and there are mysterious pagan relics in this region as well.

Boa (pronounced 'Bo'), the largest island in Lough Erne, is connected to the mainland by a bridge at either end. Its name comes from *Badhbha*, war goddess of the Ulster Celts, and a curious remnant of the pre-Christian Druidic cult can be seen in the old cemetery at **Caldragh**, signposted down a track at the island's western end. The stone idol with a face on either side, called a Janus figure, is thought to have been used in rituals.

Castle Archdale Country Park, on the shores of Lough Erne, was created from the demesne of the 18th-century Archdale manor house; only the courtyard buildings remain, housing a visitor centre and several small museums. The marina, developed as an RAF airbase during World War Two, is now a mecca for pleasure boats, and fishing trips with a ghillie can be arranged. A ferry runs to **White Island** (*every hour 1100–1800 during July–Aug, and weekends and public holidays Easter–Sept; ££*) where you can see the remains of a 12th-century church; carved into one wall are eight enigmatic figures, pagan in style but thought to belong to an earlier Christian monastery.

Castle Caldwell Forest covers an area of promontories and small islands on the western shores of Lough Erne. It is an important reserve for elusive animals such as otters and pine martens. A short trail from the car park leads through a canopy of beech trees to the derelict castle, built in 1612 and now enveloped by vines, mosses and trees – a wonderfully atmospheric spot. As you enter the grounds, notice the **Fiddler's Stone** beside the entrance arch, a memorial to Denis McCabe, a fiddler who fell from a barge and drowned in 1770. The epitaph concludes: 'On firm land only exercise your skill/There you may play and drink your fill'.

215

Marble Arch Caves

Marlbank Scenic Loop. Tel: 028 6634 8855 (booking advised). Open: Apr–Sept, daily 1000–1630 (last tour); caves may be closed after heavy rain. Tours last for 75 minutes. ££.

These spectacular caves were carved by streams running down from Cuilcagh Mountain. You can see the remarkable stalagmites, stalactites, chasms and limestone formations on a guided tour, followed by a boat ride into the dark depths. Outside the cave, the River Cladagh emerges from underground into the glen, where the 30-ft (9-m) Marble Arch stands. From here, there are fine walks further into the glen, filled with wild flowers in season. Wear comfortable shoes and a warm sweater.

Mount Stewart

A20 south of Newtownards. Tel: 028 4278 8387. House open: Easter, Apr and Oct, weekends only 1300–1800; May–Sept, Wed–Mon 1300–1800; garden open: Mar, Sun only 1400–1700; Apr–Sept, daily 1100–1800; Oct, weekends only 1100–1800; Temple of the Winds open: Apr–Oct, weekends only 1400–1700. ££.

Built in the 18th century, with later additions, Mount Stewart was the former seat of the Marquess of Londonderry. It is best known for its formal gardens, some of the finest in the British Isles. Covering 98 acres (40 hectares), they were planted with exotic plants and trees in the 1920s. The Shamrock Garden has a yew hedge in the shape of a shamrock and a topiary Irish harp; the Dodo Terrace has stone statues of dodos and an ark. The **Temple of the Winds**, a banqueting hall overlooking Strangford Lough, was built by James 'Athenian' Stuart, a pioneer of neo-classical architecture, in 1785. Highlights of the house include the dining room, with 22 chairs from the Congress of Vienna (1815) presented to Lord Castlereagh, the British foreign secretary, for his role in the talks; and a painting of the racehorse Hambletonian by George Stubbs.

Newcastle

Newcastle Tourist Information Office: Central Promenade. Tel: 028 4377 2222. Open: all year.

Newcastle is one of County Down's most popular resorts, with its 5-mile (8-km) stretch of sandy beach. There are several family attractions, including the Tropicana Pleasure Beach with water slides and a heated outdoor pool, and Coco's, an adventure playground. Automobile lovers can visit the **Route 66 American Car Museum**.

Near by is the vast and beautiful Tyrella Beach, a blue-flag beach where the **Mountains of Mourne** do seem to sweep down to the sea, as immortalised in the song by Percy French, the 19th-century lyricist. There are several well-marked paths linking the high peaks, of which Slieve Donard is the highest at 2 795ft (852m). Trail leaflets can be bought from tourist information centres in the region, including the one at Newcastle.

Portaferry

The best time to see this picturesque village on the banks of Strangford Lough is at sunset, a view that will look familiar from many brochure photographs. Its pretty waterfront, lined with terraced cottages, pubs and shops, is backed by rolling green hills. The remains of five tower houses stand on the shores around the slim channel that links the lough to the Irish Sea. Twice a day, 400 million tonnes of water flow in and out of the lough with the tides through 'the Narrows'. The lough area is a haven for marine life, with more than 2 000 species, including corals and sponges. Many can be seen at **Exploris** (*The Rope Walk; tel: 012477 28062; open: Mar–Aug, Mon–Fri 1000–1800, Sat 1100–1800, Sun 1300–1800; Sept–Feb, closing time 1700; ££*), Northern Ireland's only aquarium. A car ferry links Portaferry with Strangford (*see opposite*) on the opposite shore.

Springhill

1 mile (1.5km) from Moneymore on the Moneymore–Coagh road (B18). Tel: 028 8674 8210. Open: Apr–June and Sept, weekends and holidays 1400–1800; July–Aug, Fri–Wed 1400–1800. ££.

This whitewashed Plantation-era manor house was built in the 17th century, and has mid-18th- and early 19th-century additions. It contains family furniture, paintings and curios. The outbuildings are also of interest; one houses an important costume collection. There is a fortified barn dating from the 17th century, and two barns in the Dutch style. The grounds also contain a secluded walled garden and woodland walks.

Strangford

This pretty village lies opposite Portaferry and is the other port for the Strangford Lough car ferry. Just outside town is **Castle Ward** (*tel: 028 4488 1204; house open: Easter and June–mid-Sept, Fri–Wed 1300–1800; Apr–May and mid-Sept–Oct, weekends only 1300–1800; ££*), an 18th-century mansion with a split personality. It sports Palladian classical architecture on the front façade and Gothic on the garden side. This schizophrenic construction is the result of a dispute between Lord and Lady Bangor, who built the mansion in the 1760s. They disagreed about almost everything; the style of their house was no exception and represents a compromise. The interior design is equally mixed. There is also a Victorian laundry, a working corn mill and a pastime centre where children can dress up and play games. The 750-acre (300-hectare) estate, with beautiful walks and equestrian trails, is home to the **Strangford Lough Wildlife Centre**, with interpretative displays on the wildfowl, marine life, fauna and flora that can be seen in the area.

Cloughy Rocks lie south of Strangford, off the A2. You can often see seals here, depending on the tides. Near by are the ruins of **Kilclief Castle** and the fishing village of **Ardglass**, with no less than six castle ruins around the harbour.

Ulster American Folk Park

Mellon Road (A5), 5 miles (8km) north of Omagh. Tel: 028 8224 3292. Open: Easter–Sept, Mon–Sat 1100–1830, Sun and holidays 1130–1900; Oct–Easter, Mon–Fri 1030–1700. ££.

Plan to spend some time at this fascinating folk park which traces the history of Ulster emigrants from their pre-Famine homesteads to life in the New World. An impressive array of dwellings representing different walks of life has been superbly reconstructed, with costumed interpreters who demonstrate spinning, cooking over a turf fire and other facets of everyday life. The trail leads down an Ulster high street to the most moving exhibit in the park: an enormous coffin ship that re-creates the appalling conditions suffered by the emigrants on their Atlantic voyage. You emerge into a 19th-century streetscape of an American port town, and head on to a log cabin in the wilderness. The indoor Emigrants Exhibition, which looks at the historical background to this massive exodus and the contributions of emigrants in the New World, tells an inspirational story of the resilience of the human spirit, and is a tribute to the experience of immigrants the world over. Also in the grounds is the Centre for Migration Studies.

Ulster Folk and Transport Museum

Cultra, Holywood. Tel: 028 9042 8428. Open: July–Aug, Mon–Sat 1030–1800, Sun 1200–1800; Apr–June and Sept, Mon–Fri 0930–1700, Sat 1030–1800, Sun 1200–1800; Oct–Mar, Mon–Fri 0930–1600, Sat–Sun 1230–1630. ££.

Set in the grounds of Cultra Manor, this open-air museum – one of the best in Ireland – traces Ulster's past through a variety of reconstructed buildings. A thatched weaver's cottage, Victorian terraced houses, a rectory, a parish church, a village school and a flax mill are among the buildings that portray ways of life down the ages. There are also demonstrations of traditional crafts. The indoor transport galleries present every method of transport imaginable, from donkeys to modern aircraft. Top exhibits include the De Lorean automobile, produced in Belfast in 1982; the Irish Railway and Road Transport collections; and the exhibit on the *Titanic*, the fated luxury liner built in Belfast which sank in 1912.

Ulster History Park

7 miles (11km) north of Omagh on the B48. Tel: 028 8164 8188. Open: Apr–Sept, Mon–Sat 1030–1830, Sun 1130–1900; Oct–Mar, Mon–Fri 1030–1700; last admission 1¹/₂ hours before closing. ££.

The Ulster History Park presents a trail through time that follows Irish settlement from the prehistoric hunter-gatherers to Norman times. Full-scale constructions of hide-covered huts, *crannogs* (lake dwellings), early farms, a Plantation village and a motte and bailey fortress demonstrate how people lived, while megalithic burial tombs, an early Christian oratory, *curraghs* (small boats) and a mill show how they worked and worshipped. Events that celebrate ancient traditions are also held throughout the year.

Eating and drinking

Belfast

Madison's

59–63 Botanic Avenue. Tel: 028 9033 0040; fax: 028 9032 8007. ££.
Everything about Madison's says 'style', from the art nouveau-style doors to the amusing sculpture of a man peering out of a top-floor window. It's brilliantly located, 5 minutes' walk from the University, 10 minutes' walk from the city centre, and surrounded by good restaurants, bars and nightclubs. The spacious bar and restaurant are a feast for the eye as well as the palate, with a fantastical twisting iron staircase and ultra-modern décor. The food is excellent bistro fare – seafood, steak, poultry, pasta and vegetarian dishes with Eastern spices. Great selection of wines by the glass or bottle from 'The Collection' of their hand-picked wines.

The McCausland Hotel

34–38 Victoria Street. Tel: 028 9022 0200; fax: 028 9022 0220. £££.
Luxurious restaurant and more affordable café bar. Located near the river and clock tower, just a few minutes' stroll from the city centre.

Antica Roma

67 Botanic Avenue. Tel: 028 9031 1121. Closed Sun and Sat lunch. ££.
Amazing *trompe l'oeil* murals of a Roman villa complement the Italian dishes served with a Celtic flare. The seafood dishes are recommended.

Café Society

3 Donegall Square West. Tel: 028 9043 9525. Closed Sun, no lunch. ££.
Try to get a window table for a great view over the central square. Beautiful seafood – mixed fish grill of salmon, red snapper and grouper served with polenta. There are outdoor pavement tables in summer.

Bushmills

The Bushmills Inn

25 Main Street, Bushmills. Tel: 028 2073 2339; fax: 028 2073 2048. ££–£££. This atmospheric old coaching inn is an Ulster favourite. The main hotel was built in the 1830s, and the character of this era is evoked by the gas-lights in the Victorian bar, the flagstoned kitchen with an open turf fire, now a cosy lounge, the grand staircase, oil lamps, and the circular library with its secret room. The restaurant, with whitewashed walls and intimate snugs, looks out on to the courtyard garden. The excellent Taste of Ulster menu is prepared from fresh local produce.

Derry

Beech Hill Country House Hotel
32 Ardmore Road. Tel: 028 7134 9279; fax: 028 7134 5366. ££–£££. Just 2 miles (3km) from Derry city centre, this luxurious country house hotel is a favoured hideaway for prominent politicians, not least because of the superb Ardmore Restaurant, with a sophisticated menu prepared by a top chef. The house, with its distinctive porch and bow windows, was built in 1729 by Captain Thomas Skipton, head of a prominent Plantation family, and is set in extensive landscaped grounds with fine old beech trees, beautiful gardens, streams and a pond.

Le Café Monroe
15 Carlisle Road. £. This cheerful café, just outside the city walls on one of Derry's main shopping streets, is decked out with large black-and-white photos of Marilyn Monroe in her heyday. The blonde belle's ancestors are said to have come from nearby Limavady. The friendly proprietors serve breakfast all day, as well as sandwiches, quiches, café meals and a four-course Sunday lunch (from 1230–1730).

Downpatrick

Harry Afrika's
Lower Market Street. Tel: 028 4461 7161. £. This restaurant is open every day from early morning to late at night. It serves superb lunches, high teas and dinners, but is most famous for its Greedy Pig breakfasts. Bring your own bottle.

Newcastle

Burrendale Hotel & Country Club
51 Castlewellan Road. Tel: 028 4372 2599; fax: 028 4372 2328. ££–£££. Set beneath the Mourne Mountains just outside Newcastle, there are impressive views from this splendid hotel. Service is impressive in the Vine Restaurant, where you can choose from an excellent à la carte or *table d'hôte* menu of fresh Ulster fare and a fine wine list. The casual Cottage Kitchen has a good bistro menu; there are also two bars. Guests can use the pool, jacuzzis, saunas and fitness facilities in the Country Club.

Portaferry

The Cornstore Restaurant
Portaferry. Tel: 028 4272 9779. ££. Casual dining in the smart ground-floor bistro (open Mon–Sun 1200–2100) focuses on fresh fish, from Portavogie cod to Strangford Lough mussels, lobster and crab, with a choice of meat and vegetarian dishes as well. The first-floor restaurant (open Fri–Sat 1930–2200) has a creative menu ranging from teriyaki salmon to chargrilled vegetables with red onion marmalade. The food and service are top quality in both.

Shopping in Belfast

Belfast's grand old buildings and pedestrianised shopping streets are a shopper's delight. **Donegall Place** has many of the familiar British chain stores as well as family-owned establishments. Try **Hoggs** for crystal, china, linen and other Irish quality gifts. To the left of Donegall Place, through the **Queen's Arcade**, is the **Fountain Area**, with its multitude of speciality shops. Donegall Place becomes **Royal Avenue**, where you'll find the **Castlecourt Centre**, an indoor mall. **High Street** is another main shopping thoroughfare, with narrow 'entries' or lanes running off it. The **Spires Centre**, housed in a former Presbyterian church building, is filled with up-market designer shops.

Markets

St George's Market, on May Street, is a Friday morning food market, with the Variety Market next door. Donegall Pass, off Shaftsbury Square, has a row of antique shops and a Saturday morning flea market.

Entertainment in Belfast

You can hear all kinds of music in Belfast's pubs, from traditional Irish to country and rock, to jazz and blues. Some of the most atmospheric can be found around the **Crown Liquor Saloon** (*see page 200*). Nightclubs are also plentiful, with many located in the Golden Mile and University area. These stay open later, until 0100–0300. **The King's Hall** (*tel: 028 9066 5225*) is a major venue for rock and pop concerts. The **Empire** (*tel: 028 9032 8110*), in a former church on Botanic Avenue, has stand-up comedy as well as music. Film buffs should check out the **Queen's Film Theatre** (*tel: 028 9024 4857*), an art cinema showing foreign and independent films (closed between terms).

Listings magazines

To find out what's on where, look for the free listings papers called The Big List *and* That's Entertainment. *The* Belfast Telegraph *also has a good 'What's On' section.*

Performing arts

Belfast is a vibrant centre for the performing arts, attracting many international artists from a variety of fields. The **Belfast Festival at Queen's** is Ireland's biggest arts festival, which runs for three weeks every autumn and hosts world-class stars in theatre, dance, comedy, opera, jazz, folk and classical music. **Waterfront Hall** (*tel: 028 9033 4400*) is the city's state-of-the-art concert and conference venue. The **Grand Opera House** (*tel: 028 9024 9129*) presents drama, ballet, musicals and pantomime, as well as opera, and has hosted many of the world's top stars. **Ulster Hall** (*tel: 028 9032 3900*) is home to the Ulster Orchestra. Classical and contemporary Irish drama is featured at the **Lyric Theatre** (*tel: 028 9038 1081*).

The **Old Museum Arts Centre** (*tel: 028 9023 3332*) is at the cutting edge of theatre, dance, poetry, mime and visual arts. Permanent and temporary art exhibitions can be seen at the **Ulster Museum** and the **Ormeau Baths Gallery**.

Shopping in Derry

The Craft Village, off Shipquay Street (*tel: 01504 260329*), is a warren of craft shops and apartments where you can watch demonstrations. **Austin's**, Ireland's oldest department store, adjoins the Diamond and has a selection of quality gifts.

Entertainment in Derry

Derry has a thriving arts scene. The **Orchard Gallery** (*Orchard Street; tel: 028 7126 9675*) and the **Context Gallery** (*5–7 Artillery Street; tel: 028 7137 3538*) hold contemporary art exhibitions. Several theatre companies perform at the **Foyle Arts Centre** (*tel: 028 7126 6657*), the **Rialto Entertainment Centre** (*tel: 028 7126 0516*), **The Playhouse** (*tel: 028 7126 8027*) and **St Columb's Theatre** (*tel: 028 7126 2880*).

Tracing your ancestry

With so many descendants of Irish emigrants touring the homeland of their forebears, ancestor hunting is one of the most popular visitor activities in Ireland. Every county has a heritage or genealogical centre that can help you gain access to parish records and other data from that region. The extent of information available and the level of facilities varies from one centre to the next; some are computerised. Fees are generally charged for professional assistance, so always enquire before you begin a search.

A good starting point is the Genealogy Advisory Service at the National Library of Ireland in Dublin. Before you can begin a search, you will need to find out as much as possible about your ancestors (not simply your family name) from family records; civil records of births, deaths and marriages; church records; immigration records; and the like.

National Library, Dublin

The National Library, designed by Sir Thomas Deane and opened in 1890, now contains the excellent **Genealogy Room**, moved here from No 2 Kildare Street, which offers advice, references and computer searches for tracing your Irish ancestry (*Kildare Street; tel: 01 603 0200; open: Mon–Wed 1000–2100, Thur–Fri 1000–1700, Sat 1000–1300*).

Ulster American Folk Park

The **Centre for Migration Studies** at the Ulster American Folk Park has a reference library and emigration database for genealogical research (*for information, tel: 028 8225 6315; fax: 028 8224 2241; e-mail: uafp@iol.ie; website: www.qub.ac.uk/cms/ and www.folkpark.com; open: Mon–Fri, 0930–1630*).

Belfast

If you're tracing ancestors in Northern Ireland, the **Public Record Office** on Balmoral Avenue has some 33 miles (53km) of records dating back to the early 17th century. Visitors can carry on their own research in the reading room (*open: Mon–Fri 0915–1645, Thur 'til 2045*), 3 miles (5km) from City Hall (*tel: 028 9025 5905 or 5906*). Another source is the **Ulster Historical Foundation** (*12 College Square East; tel: 028 9033 2288; open: Mon–Fri 0930–1730*).

Derry

The genealogy centre for Derry is located in the **Calgach Centre**, Butcher Street (*tel: 028 7126 1967; open: Mon–Fri 0900–1700*).

County Meath

If you are ancestor hunting in County Meath, a helpful contact is the **Meath Heritage and Genealogy Centre** (*Mill Street; tel: 046 36633; open: Mon–Fri 0900–1700*).

County Wicklow

The Wicklow Family History Centre, housed in Wicklow's historic gaol (*tel: 0404 20126; fax: 0404 61612; open: Mon–Thur 0900–1700, Fri 0900–1600*), provides a research service for people tracing their County Wicklow ancestry.

County Mayo

If you're tracing your ancestors in County Mayo, there are two genealogical research centres that may be of help: the **Mayo North Family Heritage Centre** near Crossmolina (*tel: 096 31809*) and the **South Mayo Family Research Centre** in Ballinrobe (*tel: 092 41214*).

Lifestyles

Shopping, eating, children and nightlife in Ireland

Shopping

Quality is the hallmark of Ireland's irresistible products – crystal, textiles, fine china, knitwear, whiskey, liqueurs, farmhouse cheeses, smoked salmon. It is enduring and it doesn't come cheap, so if you're looking for something really special, prepare to dig deep. Ireland's high-quality textiles make lasting souvenirs: look for Irish linen, such as tablecloths or napkins; Carrickmacross lace; Belleek porcelain; handwoven tweeds; and handknit Aran sweaters and other woollens.

Irish lead crystal is justly prized around the world; Waterford crystal is the best known, but it's worth considering lesser-known glassware produced in Galway, Cork, Dublin, Tipperary and Tyrone.

Then there are the more unusual items, such as ornaments made from compressed peat, polished Mourne granite or Connemara marble. For the friend who has everything (and preferably lives alone), how about an Irish pipe with a booklet on how to play it and some traditional Irish tunes? Musical instruments also make a great purchase, as do reproductions of Celtic jewellery. When in Galway, look for Claddagh friendship rings.

The larger tourist shops, such as the **House of Ireland** and **Blarney Woollen Mills**, sell a range of goods from around the country. **Avoca Handweavers** has several branches, as does **Quills** in western Ireland. Here you will find plenty of affordable choices if you want to lower your sights a little – tea cloths, table mats, T-shirts, key rings, ornaments and masses of novelty and fun items. There tends to be a shamrock-with-everything aspect, but the recipients will at least remember where the gift came from. Also look out for small local craft workshops, where you'll find unique items of pottery, ceramics and other goods. Many towns have weekly markets that can be fun places to browse.

Dublin's shopping experience

Dublin has some fine department stores selling such items as Irish pewterware mugs in exquisite designs, linen which will last for ever and distinctively crafted jewellery with a Celtic influence.

Spend time in **Clery's** in O'Connell Street and **Arnott's** in Henry Street. Both have dedicated Irish shops within the store. Wander around **Brown Thomas** in Grafton Street, where everything from a velvet scarf to a cocktail shaker has a classy look.

Beautiful Irish crafts, including Waterford crystal, bone china, jewellery and textiles attract visitors to the **House of Ireland** in Nassau Street near Trinity College. Those who couldn't make up their minds in the shop have a second chance as they leave for home from Dublin Airport – the company has a branch in the departure hall.

Many people head for pedestrianised Grafton Street first. This is the exciting core of the city's shopping experience, and it's handy for other main streets. One of the joys of shopping in Dublin compared with most European capitals is that it's compact and manageable while offering a good variety of shops, boutiques and other retail outlets.

For high fashion, Grafton Street and its environs certainly won't let you down, and for the mass market there's **Marks & Spencer**.

Even in the dead of winter the flower stalls are piled high with glorious blooms, and there's nearly always a busker somewhere, playing the fiddle expertly or singing his heart out. It's a place with a joyous atmosphere, and whatever intentions you start out with you'll find yourself in a what-the-hell spending mood.

At the southern end of Grafton Street, **St Stephen's Green Shopping Centre** stands like a multi-decked cruise ship. Specialist shops, places to eat, fashions for the young set (and others), fancy goods – there's something on the three floors to appeal to everyone. On the ground floor is an enormous **Dunne's**, a good-value store with 100 branches throughout the country. Clothes for

the whole family, food, drink and much more can be bought here. Take a look at **The Donegal Shop** on the top floor with its fine selection of hand-woven tweed jackets for men and women, homespun tweed caps and hats, traditional hand-knitted polo sweaters and hand-loomed Aran cardigans and sweaters in 100 per cent wool.

Another of Dublin's prestigious shopping centres is the **Powerscourt Townhouse** in William Street South. Converted from a Georgian mansion in the 1980s, it still has the original mahogany staircase. Antiques and art works, clothing, jewellery and other goods provide pleasurable browsing and buying, and there are places to relax over coffee or tea.

Kennedy and McSharry, in Nassau Street, has been a noted menswear shop for more than a century, and a few doors away at **Kevin and Howlien** you can buy a length of tweed or ready-made jackets for men and women.

The **Jervis Centre**, off Henry Street, is useful for fashion shopping. For general shopping away from the city centre, malls can be found in most of Dublin's suburbs.

Indoor market

People with an eye for the unusual and those who are natural born collectors should make a weekend beeline for **Mother Redcap's Market** (*open: Fri, Sat and Sun 1000–1730*). Although it's all indoors, the booths line little streets. All sorts of bric-à-brac, antiques and collectables and general flea-market discoveries are on sale. There are old photographs, good knitwear, furniture, mats, nails and screws, electrical items, paintings, gadgets and heaven knows what. Mother Redcap's is in an old brick building in Back Lane, across Cornmarket from St Audoen's Church. The entrance is fairly inconspicuous. If you can't find it, you'll know you're getting warm when you hear the music.

" *I live in County Clare. I draw back my curtains every morning and see County Clare. Now why would I want a picture of County Clare?* "

Woman to man selling paintings in Mother Redcap's Market

Temple Bar

If you're looking for contemporary Irish art – and there's some impressive talent about – you should stroll around **Arthouse**, a multimedia arts centre in Curved Street. It costs nothing to look, and you can buy if you want to, choosing from some 4 000 works, or perhaps commissioning an artist (*tel: 01 605 6800; open: Mon–Fri 0900–1830, Sat 1000–1800; Temple Bar Information Centre: 18 Eustace Street, Temple Bar, Dublin 2; tel: 01 671 5717*).

Shop opening hours in Dublin's centre are generally Mon–Sat 0900–1800 (to 2000 on Thur). In the suburbs Friday is the usual late opening night. Some of the major city centre stores now open for six hours on a Sunday, usually between 1200 and 1800.

Eating out

You will find meals to suit all tastes and budgets in Ireland, from superb table d'hôte *dining in country-house hotels to simple but filling café fare. Though the tradition of eating a large meal at midday is shifting with the times, big breakfasts such as the Ulster fry (bacon, sausage, egg, grilled tomato, black pudding, potato cake and soda farl) are still the norm.*

Pub lunches are excellent value, with tasty dishes that range from soup and sandwiches to full meals or a carvery. Many pubs also serve evening meals. In Northern Ireland families tend to have high tea – a light cooked meal – around 1800. Ethnic restaurants serving a variety of cuisine, and pizza, pasta and fast-food chains, are on the rise. Fish and chips, an Irish favourite, are also a good budget option.

Traditional foods

Among the traditional dishes to try are **Dublin coddle**, a supper dish made with chopped sausages, ham

or bacon cooked in a stock with potatoes and onions; and boxty, a potato pancake stuffed with marinated beef, chicken or other fillings

A good **Irish stew** is worth tracking down. It usually comes with nice chunky carrots and possibly pearl barley. Purists will tell you that if it has anything but layers of neck of lamb, onions and potatoes with herbs, stock and seasoning, it isn't authentic Irish stew. But who's going to complain about a few carrots as long as it's cooked long and slowly to thicken up the juices?

One delectable dish that appears on many restaurant menus is **beef in Guinness**, or any other Irish stout. It's a simple casserole of cubed steak, onions, mushrooms and stout, and according to one Dublin chef, a little soft brown sugar works wonders for the flavour.

Pheasant, partridge, venison, hare and wild duck appear on many Irish menus. The humble rabbit, enjoyed casseroled or in a pie in Irish homes, rarely makes it to the city's dining

Where to eat

The Northern Ireland Tourist Board publishes Where to Eat in Northern Ireland, *a comprehensive booklet listing restaurants, cafés, pubs and hotels, price brackets and type of food served. It is sold at newsagents and tourist information offices. The Irish Tourist Board publishes a similar booklet,* Dining in Ireland, *but food lovers would do well to invest in a copy of the now-legendary* Bridgestone Irish Food Guide, *which is a near-comprehensive guide to all the best food shops, markets, cafés, restaurants and farm shops in the land.*

establishments, which is a pity considering its low cholesterol, tender flesh and subtle flavour.

Roast duck, cooked crisply, plump chickens which have foraged around farmyard and field, pork from rootling pigs and the finest hams, smoked to perfection or left 'green' – these farm-reared meats, cooked without embellishment, have given the cuisine of modern Ireland a high reputation.

Bread and potatoes

Irish breads and sweets, including scones, barm brack (a fruity bread) and porter cake (made with dried fruit and stout) are also delicious. Irish **soda bread** is made from a yeastless dough in which buttermilk or sour milk, rolled oats and bicarbonate of soda are used. The dough is shaped into a round and a deep cross cut into it, so that when it's baked you get four plump quarters. It takes little time to prepare, needs no proving and bakes in about 45 minutes, so it can be cooked in time for breakfast – it really does need to be eaten fresh.

Boxty is another speciality – bread made with potatoes, some mashed, some grated, and flour. Very filling, very tasty. It's served warm, in the form of well-risen rounds, spread with butter.

Potatoes, of course, have traditionally been the mainstay of the Irish diet, and Irish cooks have some special ways with them. They jazz up mashed potatoes by adding chopped spring onions (scallions) to them and call it **champ**. Ideally, the spring onions should be simmered in a little milk before mixing them, with the milk, into the potatoes. Sometimes fresh chopped chives, uncooked, are used instead of spring onions.

Potato soup, perfectly seasoned, is another dish in which the Irish excel. Potato and leek soup, and potato and parsley soup, are hearty and sustaining choices and it is extremely rare to come across any soup in a pub or restaurant that is less than perfect.

They may not be exactly what the doctor ordered, but if you have a heavy sightseeing session ahead of you, **potato cakes** with your meal will prevent flagging. They're made from a mixture of mashed potatoes and finely chopped cooked cabbage and a powdering of flour, all blended together over a low heat in a little boiled milk with bacon fat added. And that's not all! The mixture is moulded into cakes and fried in more bacon fat.

" *Eat fish, live longer.*
Eat oysters, love longer. **"**
Advertising slogan of the seafood kitchen at Johnny Fox's pub at Glencullen in the Dublin Mountains

Drinking

Ireland's most famous brew is **Guinness**, a dark, heavy beer with a thick creamy head. The locals call it 'stout'. The taste and texture of stout depends on how it is stored – and poured. A good pint can't be hurried, so enjoy the ritual. Other Irish beers include Murphys, a slightly sweeter stout; Kilkenny and Smithwicks. Stout is often drunk with Ireland's other famous drink, whiskey (note the 'e' in the spelling), and in country pubs you'll hear the locals ordering 'a pint and a drop' or 'a bottle and a half 'un'.

Bushmills in Northern Ireland claims to be the world's oldest legal whiskey distillery. Other leading brands include Jamesons and Powers. Irish whiskey must be matured in wooden casks for at least seven years before it is bottled, and its flavour is distinct from its Scottish, American and Canadian counterparts. You might also want to try the whiskey-based liqueurs, Irish Mist and Bailey's Irish Cream.

237

Ireland with children

With over 60 per cent of Ireland's population under the age of 25, children won't lack for company. The Irish love children and welcome them in hotels and restaurants with few exceptions. Most hotels can provide a cot for infants, with advance notice, and many can arrange baby-sitting services. Restaurants often have children's menus. Children are allowed to enter pubs until around 1730 (sometimes a bit later if the pub isn't busy), although they cannot drink alcohol until the age of 18. Theme parks and other attractions geared for children are mentioned throughout the guidebook; many places offer family tickets. When booking hotels and public transport, be sure to ask about any children's discounts and the age limit; these can add up to considerable savings.

Dublin for children

Although very much a city for adults, Dublin has plenty to amuse and stimulate younger visitors in or near the city.

Talk to the animals

Dublin Zoo, in Phoenix Park, has enough to occupy a child's attention for hours: a jolly train ride, a pet-care section, play areas for little ones, a discovery centre and all the animals. There's a World of Primates, with chimpanzees, spider monkeys and other species on islands in a large lake, and a section of cold-climate creatures – polar bears, arctic foxes and snowy owls. Many rare animals and birds can be seen. *Tel: 01 677 1425. Open: Mon–Sat 0930–1800, Sun 1030–1800. Earlier closing in winter. Family ticket available.*

Waxing lyrical

Small children will be enchanted to find themselves amid familiar characters in the World of Fairytales and Fantasy at the **National Wax Museum** (*see page 44*). Older ones will enjoy shuddering at ghastly encounters in the Chamber of Horrors and meeting such stars as Madonna and Elvis in the flesh – well, almost. *Granby Row, Parnell Square, Dublin 1. Tel: 01 872 6340. Open: Mon–Sat 1000–1730, Sun 1200–1730. ££; concessions.*

Where Dublin began

Sail a stormy sea as the Norsemen did 1 000 years ago and land in the Viking settlement of Dyflin. Here you are invited into a Viking home to hear from the occupant what everyday life was like. Although the time travel aspect of Dublin's **Viking Adventure** has general interest, it has particular appeal for children, especially those who will enjoy banter with the Norse sea captain. There's a cleverly presented cross-section of Dublin through the ages, with Viking Dyflin at the base. A museum and gift shop complete the experience. *Essex Street West, Temple Bar, Dublin 8. Tel: 01 679 6040. Open: Tue–Sat 1000–1630. ££; concessions.*

Arts at the Ark

The Ark is a cultural centre for children which holds workshops, concerts, art and other exhibitions and presents performances in its

own theatre, all designed to appeal to 4- to 14-year-olds. You'll need to book and to check on what programmes are scheduled during your stay. *Eustace Street, opposite Temple Bar Information Centre, Temple Bar. Tel: 01 670 7788. Open: Tue–Fri 0930–1600.*

Paddle your own...

With all equipment supplied, no previous experience necessary and qualified instructors in attendance, you can enjoy **Dublin Bay by kayak**. A mini-bus picks you up at the Suffolk Street tourist centre, returning three hours later. Pre-booking is essential. *Adventure Activities, 5 Tritonville Avenue, Sandymount, Dublin 4. Tel: 01 668 8047. Trips available: Mon 1630, Thur 1000, Fri 1900. Family ticket available.*

Rock and burgers

Rock 'n' roll memorabilia, including guitars signed by rock stars and U2's original drum kit, can be seen at **Captain America's**, where they serve more than a dozen types of burger. *44 Grafton Street, Dublin 2. Tel: 01 671 5266. Open: daily, noon–midnight.*

239

After dark

Ireland is a nation of performers. You can book a ticket for an orchestral concert or see something classical at the theatre. Or you can be chatting with the locals in a pub and suddenly there's a party. Someone has brought his fiddle along, someone else joins in with a bodhràn *– a small goatskin drum – or a tin whistle, feet begin to tap and a session has begun.*

The pub

The pub is the centre of Irish social life, much more than a mere venue for downing a pint. In days gone by, marriage agreements and business deals were sealed here, and it's still the place for courting, singing, playing music and, most of all, enjoying the *craic* (pronounced 'crack'), an Irish word meaning fun and entertainment.

'Singing pubs' are simply places where impromptu music sessions break out and everyone joins in; don't worry if you don't know the words to the Irish ballads –

contemporary folk and country tunes are part of the standard repertoire. Some of the best *craic* can be had at small, smoky local hangouts where visitors are welcome but not catered for. Large tourist-orientated venues exist in the main centres.

In cities, seek out the old-style Victorian pubs with ornate décor and 'snugs', private booths designed to afford privacy to genteel womenfolk. In rural areas, you'll still find pubs that function as a sort of general store. There's no better place for people-watching, and you don't have to drink alcohol to enjoy the atmosphere. Many pubs now serve food at lunchtime, or coffee and tea during the day.

Festivals

Festivals and fairs are held year-round throughout the country, with most taking place between March and October. Many are dedicated to music, dancing, literature and the arts, such as Dublin's theatre festival or Wexford's opera festival; others are local harvest festivals or livestock fairs, such as Clarenbridge's oyster festival and Killorglin's Puck Fair. Other famous gatherings include the matchmaking festival at Lisdoonvarna and the Rose of Tralee festival. The regional and national tourist boards publish a Calendar of Events.

Dublin clubs

One of Dublin's liveliest nightclubs is **The Kitchen** in the Clarence Hotel at Wellington Quay. It is owned by U2, who have resurrected the 1920s hotel. Most of the nightclubs are in Leeson Street, off St Stephen's Green. The **Burlington Hotel** in Upper Leeson Street features a classy Irish cabaret. The snappy dressers among the young set dance the night away at **The PoD** in Harcourt Street.

For dancing to music from the 1960s, 1970s and 1980s, try the **Leftbank Bar** in Anglesea Street, Temple Bar. **La Med**, in Essex Street, Temple Bar, has a jazz bar. Irish music sessions and dancing nights are held at **Lanigan's Pub** at the Clifton Court Hotel, O'Connell's Bridge, where turf fires and candlelight set the mood.

The brother of rock singer Bono owns the **Tosca Restaurant** in Suffolk Street. Visiting musicians go there and it's popular with actors. Bono himself, so they say, is sometimes seen in **The Dockers Pub** at Sir John Rogerson's Quay, near the Windmill Lane Studio. Sing-alongs are held here, and also

Listings

Keep an eye on the major daily newspapers for details of what's on. The fortnightly Hot Press *gives the low-down on the music scene. Regulars on the Dublin calendar are the Film Festival in March, the three-day Guinness Blues Festival in late July and the two-week Dublin Theatre Festival in October.*

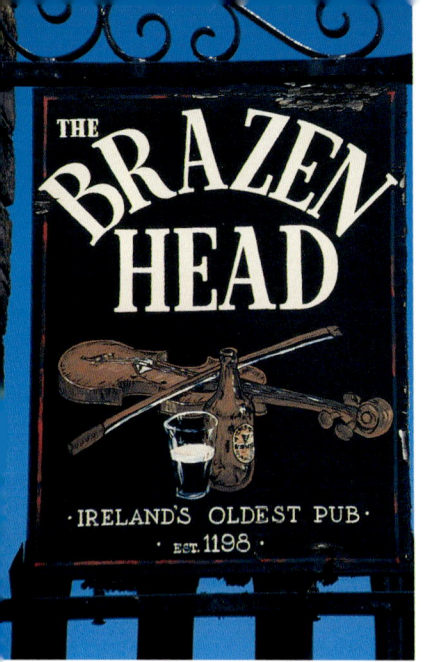

Theatre, in Lower Abbey Square, is noted for its Irish classics and (in the Peacock) the work of new writers. Contemporary works are staged at the **Gate Theatre**, Parnell Square. Performances of general and family appeal are presented at the **Gaiety Theatre**, South King Street, where dance, drama, opera and musicals take place. The **Olympia Theatre** in Dame Street stages music events and family entertainment.

Venues for experimental theatre include the **Andrews Lane Theatre**, the Tivoli in Francis Street and the **Project Arts Centre**, East Essex Street. Classical music is performed at the **National Concert Hall**, and the occasional gig is held there.

at the **Brazen Head**, where Irish music nights are a regular feature.

Out-of-town spots that Dubliners love include the Abbey Tavern at **Howth**, where great Irish entertainment is staged, and Johnny Fox's Pub at **Glencullen**. They have 'hooley' nights with ballad singers and the Fox's Irish Dancing Troupe. Another is **Polly Hops**, a venerable inn and restaurant at Newcastle, southwest of Dublin. As well as impromptu sessions, there are party nights with singing, dancing and story-telling.

Performing arts

Dublin takes great pride in its performing arts. The **Abbey Theatre**, incorporating the smaller Peacock

Ghosts and ghouls

For a mobile form of drama, join the **Trapeze Theatre Company** in a nocturnal *Walk Macabre Murder*, during which the supernatural and other horrors are enacted at some of the city's scenes of violence and evil.

Other after-dark spine-chillers are the **Dublin Ghost Bus Tour**, which takes you to scenes of body-snatching, hauntings and Dracula's Dublin connections and, in the comfort of the Legal Eagle Tavern, you are introduced to the superstitions of a traditional Irish wake. The **Zosimus Experience** is another ghoulish tour, conducted on foot through the cobblestones of medieval Dublin.

Comedy, cinemas and dogs

After that, how about a good laugh? Comedy theatre is increasingly enlivening the entertainment scene and the **Tivoli Theatre** is one venue. Irish and international stand-up comedians dispense hilarity at **Murphy's Laughter Lounge** at Eden Quay, O'Connell Bridge.

Dublin's many cinemas in the centre and suburbs offer cheaper seats before 1700. The giant-screen **IMAX Experience** and the nine-screen **Virgin Cinema** are both in the Parnell Centre, Parnell Street – an ultra-modern entertainment centre with family attractions, themed bars and restaurants.

Fancy a flutter? There's **greyhound racing** on Mon, Tue and Fri evenings at Harold's Cross.

Tickets

Tickets and information on most events, theatres, shows and tours are available from the Ticket Desk, Dublin Tourism Centre, Suffolk Street, Dublin 2. For ticket reservations by credit card, tel: 01 605 7777.

" *Once I asked a Dublin policeman to tell me the exact time ... and he replied at once without the ghost of a smile that the exact time was between two and three.* "

Honor Tracey

243

Practical information

245

Practical information

Accommodation

Accommodation in Ireland ranges from luxurious castles to horse-drawn caravans. You'll find large purpose-built hotels as well as renovated historic buildings with modern amenities. 'You're very welcome' is a greeting you'll hear at most guesthouses and bed-and-breakfast accommodation; it's a heartfelt sentiment. This is where you'll experience Ireland's legendary hospitality and get to know its people, often over a tray of tea and homemade scones.

Hotels range from atmospheric village inns to modern city properties, stately country houses to grand castles. Rates vary depending on location, time of year and the attributes of the individual properties. They are classified from one to five stars.

Guesthouses offer an informal atmosphere in Victorian and Georgian houses, large family homes, or modern buildings. They are rated separately, from one to four stars.

Irish Homes and Farmhouses
accommodation (B&B) gives you a
chance to experience daily life with an
Irish family, in traditional cottages,
bungalows, farmhouses and other
homes located in towns, villages
and the countryside.

Be Our Guest, the Irish Hotels
Federation (*13 Northbrook Road,
Dublin 6; tel: 01 497 6459; fax:
01 497 4613; www.beourguest.ie*)
provides information on hotels
and guesthouses.

Gulliver *tel: 0800 668 668 66* in
the Republic; in Northern Ireland
tel: 0800 783 5740. Tourist
information and reservations.

Tourist information offices operate
a nation-wide accommodation booking
service for visitors.

Airports

Belfast International Airport (*tel:
028 9442 2888*) is 18 miles (29km)
from the city centre. A half-hourly
Airbus service runs to the main bus
and rail stations in the city; journey
time is 30 minutes.

Belfast City Airport (*tel: 028 9045
7745*) is just 4 miles (6.5km) away.
Bus no 21 leaves for the main bus
depot every half an hour and takes
about ten minutes.

Dublin Airport (*tel: 01 844 4900*) lies
6 miles (10km) north of the city. **Airlink**,
a 30-minute express **bus** service, leaves
every 20 minutes for the main bus and
rail stations in the city.

Cork Airport (*tel: 021 313131*)
also has an express **bus** service, Bus
Éireann, taking 15 minutes to get into

the city. Buses leave every 45 minutes
on weekdays and hourly at weekends.

Climate

Ireland is one of the wettest countries
in Europe with the west receiving the
most rain. April is generally the driest
month, though rainfall figures are
fairly steady throughout the year.
One of the amazing things about this
climate is how quickly it changes –
you can get soaked in a downpour one
minute and have bright blue skies the
next – so be prepared when you set
out for the day. In areas such as the
Ring of Kerry, where clear skies make
all the difference to the scenery, it's
a good idea to build 'rain' days into
your schedule so you can wait out
any storms. The southeast gets the
most sunshine, Northern Ireland
the least. Even in high summer, it's
never unbearably hot. Winter is mild
throughout the country.

Currency

As a member of the European Union, the Republic of Ireland's national currency became the **Euro** in 1999. However, these notes and coins are unlikely to be in circulation until 2002.

In the Republic, the unit of currency is the **Irish punt** (pronounced 'poont'). In Northern Ireland, the currency is the **pound sterling**. Both are divided into 100 pence; they come in denominations of £50, £20, £10 and £5 notes; and coins of £1, 50p, 20p, 10p, 5p, 2p and 1p.

The best exchange rates can be found at banks and *bureaux de change*. **Automatic Teller Machines** (cashpoints) are widespread. Most major **credit cards** are accepted in hotels, restaurants, petrol stations and larger shops; you will need cash for small hotels and farmhouse stays.

Customs regulations

Duty-free allowances for goods into Ireland from outside the EU are: 200 cigarettes or 100 cigarillos or 50 cigars or 250gm tobacco; two litres of table wine; one litre of spirits or two litres of fortified or sparkling wine or two litres of additional still table wine; 60ml perfume; 250ml toilet water; other dutiable goods to the value of IR£73 (£145 in Northern Ireland).

Duty-free goods are not available when travelling between the Republic and Northern Ireland. Duty-free sales for inter-community (EU) travellers were abolished in 1999.

For bringing goods home, duty-free allowances vary from country to country. Check with your travel agent or customs authority.

Electricity

Power throughout Ireland is 220 volts AC (50 cycles). **Plugs** are the same as those in the UK, with three square pins.

Entry formalities

British citizens born in the United Kingdom do not require a passport to enter Ireland. However, it is a good idea to carry **identification**. Citizens of the European Union, Australia, Canada, New Zealand, South Africa and the United States need **passports** (but not visas), which must have a minimum of six months' validity. Nationals of other countries may require an entry **visa**. Check with the Irish Embassy in your country.

Health

There are no unusual health hazards in Ireland – except perhaps midges. **Insect repellent** is useful, particularly in boggy areas. Apart from the usual over-the-counter remedies, you will need a doctor's prescription to obtain **medicines**, so it is best to bring what you need from home.

EU citizens are eligible for **medical treatment** in Ireland under the EU's social security regulations, provided you see a general practitioner who has an agreement with the Irish Health Board. Take identification and clarify your eligibility. Visitors from countries other than Britain are advised to bring an E111 form. Fees are charged for visits to the doctor's surgery in Ireland.

Information

The **Irish Tourist Board** (Bord Fáilte) (*Baggot Street Bridge, Dublin 2; tel: 01 602 4000; fax: 01 602 4100; website www.ireland.travel.ie*) and the **Northern Ireland Tourist Board** (*59 North Street, Belfast BT1 1NB; tel: 028 9024 6609; fax: 028 9024 0960; e-mail: general.enquiries.nitb@nics.gov.uk; website www.ni-tourism.com*) operate local and regional offices throughout Ireland. For information on planning your trip, contact the Irish Tourist Board offices in your country or the following regional offices:

Belfast: *53 Castle Street; tel: 028 9032 7888; fax: 028 9024 0201.*

UK: *150 New Bond Street, London W1Y 0AQ; tel: 020 7493 3201; fax: 020 7493 9065,* and *135 Buchanan Street, 1st floor, Glasgow G1 2JA; tel: 0141 204 4454; fax: 0141 204 4033.*

Other useful websites include *www.browseireland.com* and *www.tourismresources.ie*

Insurance

Unless you are a UK or EU citizen, you are advised to take out **medical insurance**, as you will be expected to pay for treatment if you fall ill. **Travel insurance** covering theft or loss of luggage, travel delays, etc, is always a good idea. Check your home contents policy to see if you are covered while travelling abroad.

Maps

Unless you plan to stick to the main national roads, it is advisable to have a detailed map. The *Ordnance Survey Road Atlas of Ireland* is recommended and is available at major booksellers. Many of the larger local tourist offices also have a selection of maps.

249

Opening times

Banks Republic of Ireland: Mon–Fri 1000–1600. Northern Ireland: Mon–Fri 0930–1630. In villages, banks may close for lunch and may not open every day.

Most **post offices** are open Mon–Fri 0900–1730 and Sat 0900–1300. Larger ones are open Mon–Sat 0800–2000 and Sun 1000–1800.

Shops Mon–Sat 0900–1730 or 1800. Smaller towns may close early on one day. Many towns and most shopping centres have late-night shopping until 2000 or 2100 on Thursdays or Fridays. In larger cities, some supermarkets are now open on Sundays 1200–1800.

Pubs and bars In the Republic, Mon–Sat 1030–2330 (some pubs close for lunch), Sun 1230–1400 and 1600–2300. In Northern Ireland, Mon–Sat 1130–2300, Sun 1230–2200.

Restaurants Lunch is generally served from 1200–1430 and dinner from 1830–2200.

Tourist offices are generally open from 0900 or 1000–1730, with longer hours in summer. Most are closed on Sunday, except in the high season. Many of the smaller local tourist offices are seasonal and are only open from Apr or May to Sept.

Heritage sites and museums In the larger cities and towns, sites are open year-round. Some of the smaller, rural museums, as well as historic houses and castles, have reduced opening hours, or may be closed altogether, in the winter.

Public holidays

New Year's Day (1 January), St Patrick's Day (17 March), Christmas Day (25 December) and St Stephen's Day (26 December) are public holidays. If they fall on a weekend, Monday or Tuesday are given in lieu and banks, shops and other services are generally closed. In the Republic, the first Monday of May, June and August and the last Monday in October are also public holidays. Although Good Friday is not an official public holiday, it is observed in most parts of Ireland.

In Northern Ireland, Easter Monday, the first and last Mondays in May, Orangeman's Day (mid-July), and the last Monday in August are observed in addition to the four main public holidays.

Reading

James Joyce is almost certainly the first name to spring into most people's minds when they think of literary Ireland. *Ulysses* is, of course, the classic, but it is hard going.

Other well-known Anglo-Irish literary names that you will recognise are the satirist **Jonathan Swift**, who wrote *Gulliver's Travels*; the creator of society plays such as *The Importance of Being Earnest*, **Oscar Wilde**; the dramatist **George Bernard Shaw**, author of *St Joan* and *Pygmalion*; the melancholic poet **W B Yeats** and the novelist and playwright **Samuel Beckett** of *Waiting for Godot* fame.

Safety and security

Ireland is generally a safe place to visit, but you should take normal precautions against petty crime. Do not carry your passport or large amounts of cash or valuables around on the street. Mind your wallet or handbag in crowds and never leave cameras, bags or luggage unattended, especially in cars.

If your passport is lost or stolen, the main foreign embassies are located in Dublin, and there is an American consulate in Belfast. Emergency telephone numbers for the police (*Garda* in Irish), fire and ambulance services are 999 or 112.

Contemporary authors who have scaled the giddy heights of world fame include **Maeve Binchy** (*Light a Penny Candle, Tara Road*), **Roddy Doyle** (*The Commitments, Paddy Clarke Ha Ha Ha*), **Frank McCourt** with his autobiographical works *Angela's Ashes* (now a film as well) and *'Tis*. **Séamus Heaney** was awarded the Nobel Prize for Literature in 1995 and has recently won several literary awards for his translation of *Beowulf*.

For **history** buffs, try *A Concise History of Ireland* by Máire and Conor Cruise O'Brien.

Telephones

To telephone Ireland from abroad, dial your international access code, plus 353 (Ireland's national code), plus the area code (omitting the initial zero), then the number. The national code for Northern Ireland is 44. When dialling Northern Ireland from the Republic, dial 08 before the local number. If you want to call abroad from Ireland, the international prefix is 00 (plus the country code, area code and local number you wish to dial). Calls are cheaper between 1800 and 0800.

251

Pay phones are widely available throughout Ireland. Phonecards range from £2 to £16, and are sold at post offices and newsagents. There are also plenty of pay phones in bars and shops.

If you need operator assistance to make a call, dial 10 for Ireland and the UK and 114 for an international call. Directory enquiries: 1190 for Ireland, 1197 for the UK and 1198 for international enquiries.

Time

All of Ireland is on Greenwich Mean Time (GMT), which is the same as in the United Kingdom. Clocks go forward one hour for daylight saving in the summer.

Tipping

If service is not already included in your bill, the standard tip in restaurants is 10 per cent (up to 15 per cent for particularly good service). Tip taxi drivers about 10 per cent of the metered fare, but hackney cabs who drive for prearranged sums do not expect tips. Tipping is not expected by bar staff in pubs, or for hotel services such as serving a drink or carrying bags to your room – if in doubt, a small tip will suffice.

Toilets

If you learn no other words of Irish, remember that *Fir* means 'men' and *Mna* means 'women'. When looking for the public toilets in Gaeltacht areas, the word is *Leithris*. If there are no public toilets, you can generally use the facilities in a pub or hotel, although you will be expected to buy a drink.

Travellers with disabilities

More and more hotels and guesthouses are providing facilities for travellers with disabilities. You can request a fact sheet that lists suitable establishments by county from the **National Rehabilitation Board** (*Access Dept, 25 Clyde Road, Dublin 4; tel: 01 608 0400; fax: 01 668 5029*).

Many tourist sights throughout Ireland now have access for wheelchairs, but it would be wise to check by telephone before setting off.

Buses in Dublin are not equipped to accommodate disabled passengers, and many train stations are difficult. The *InterCity Guide for Mobility Impaired Passengers*, available at any railway station, details the easiest access at stations nation-wide.

253

Index

Editorial, design and production credits

Project management: Dial House Publishing Services

Series editor: Christopher Catling

Copy editor: Kate Owen

Proof-reader: Janet Wiltshire

Series and cover design: Trickett & Webb Limited

Cover artwork: Wenham Arts

Text layout: Wenham Arts

Map work: Polly Senior

Repro and image setting: Z2 Repro, Thetford, Norfolk, UK

Printed and bound by: Artes Graficas ELKAR S. Coop.

Acknowledgements

We would like to thank the following photographers and organisations for the photographs used in this book, to whom the copyright in the photographs belongs:

Bord Failte Photo: pages 102, 103, 104, 105, 106, 169,

Caroline Jones: pages 4, 6, 19, 20, 114, 119, 120, 125, 127, 129, 132, 175, 240, 242, 244 and 246.

Christopher Hill: pages 78, 79, 91, 100, 101, 121, 134, 149, 160, 162, 163, 170, 171, 172, 183, 188, 190, 191, 200, 208, 209, 211, 216, 218 and 219.

Donna Dailey: pages 62, 71, 73, 74, 84, 97, 112, 113, 122, 131, 139, 145, 146, 150, 156, 164, 167, 176, 181, 185, 186, 194, 199, 203, 205, 207, 213, 215 and 220.

Image Select International: page 99

J Allen Cash: page 95.

Larry Dunmire: pages 11, 13, 14, 16, 25, 26, 28, 31, 37, 38, 40, 42, 44, 51, 56, 57, 58, 65, 67A, 67B, 69, 76, 89, 92, 97, 109, 111, 140, 153, 155, 193, 228, 232, 233, 235, 237, 238, 247, 248, 249 and 251.

Neil Setchfield: pages 9, 12, 17, 33, 34, 46, 49, 227, 230, 234, 239, 242, 252 and 253.

Spectrum: page 83.